Rising Wage Inequality
The 1980s Experience
in Urban Labor Markets

Thomas Hyclak

2000

W.E. Upjohn Institute for Employment Research
Kalamazoo, Michigan

Library of Congress Cataloging-in-Publication Data

Hyclak, Thomas.
    Rising wage inequality: the 1980s experience in urban labor markets / Thomas Hyclak.
        p. cm.
    Includes bibliographical references and index.
    ISBN 0-88099-208-5 (cloth : alk. paper)—ISBN 0-88099-207-7 (paper : alk. paper)
        1. Wages—United States.   2. Wages—United States—Regional disparities.
    3. Wages—Effect of education on—United States.   4. Labor market—
    United States.   5. Employee fringe benefits—United States.   I. Title.

HD4975 .H929 2000
331.2′973—dc21   00-031996

Copyright 2000
W.E. Upjohn Institute for Employment Research
300 S. Westnedge Avenue
Kalamzaoo, Michigan 49007-4686

Cover design by J.R. Underhill.
Index prepared by Diane Worden.
Printed in the United States of America.

I dedicate "my story" to Jean, Anna, and Ben.

Contents

List of Figures

List of Tables

viii

Acknowledgments

I sincerely thank the W.E. Upjohn Institute for Employment Research for providing financial support for the research described in this monograph. I am also grateful for financial support from the Martindale Center for the Study of Private Enterprise at Lehigh University. Without such support this labor-intensive project would not have been possible.

I received helpful comments and assistance with the data from Anthony Barkume, Tim Bartik, and Alan Krueger. Jonathan Ohn provided excellent research assistance. I am indebted to the staff of the E.W. Fairchild-Martindale Library at Lehigh University, in particular to Roseanne Bowerman, Sally McIntosh, Barbara Parenti, and Pat Ward, for their help in getting the project off the ground. I also appreciate greatly the professional assistance of Diane Oechsle and Rene Hollinger in producing this report.

The Author

Thomas Hyclak is Professor of Economics and Chair of the Economics Department at Lehigh University. Born in Cleveland, Ohio, he received B.A. and M.A. degrees from Cleveland State University and a Ph.D. in Economics from the University of Notre Dame. He taught briefly at Ball State University before joining the Lehigh faculty in 1979. Professor Hyclak's research has concentrated largely on empirical studies of the performance of urban and regional labor markets. His published work includes examinations of the effect of unions on urban wage and income inequality, the determinants of inter-area differences in cyclical and noncyclical unemployment, the causes and consequences of real wage rigidity in local labor markets, the impact of structural change in labor demand on local unemployment, and the interaction between labor and housing markets over the business cycle. He lives in Bethlehem, Pennsylvania, with his wife Jean, daughter Anna, and son Ben.

1 Introduction

One of the most significant labor market developments in the last decade and a half has been the sharp rise in wage inequality in the United States, the United Kingdom, and many other countries. For example, Karoly (1988) estimated the variance in the logarithm of annual earnings for white males working at least 35 hours a week and 50 weeks a year at 0.282 in 1969, 0.264 in 1979, and 0.376 in 1987. The 42 percent increase from 1979 to 1987 brought that measure of wage inequality to levels unseen in the United States since the 1930s (Goldin and Margo 1992).

A change of such magnitude has not escaped the attention of economists, particularly given the social and political consequences of rising wage inequality. A substantial body of literature on the subject, with contributions by almost every prominent labor economist, has emerged over the past decade. That literature, reviewed briefly in the next section, has sharpened our understanding of many dimensions of the changing wage structure in the United States and other countries.[1] However, there are still many questions about the causes of the abrupt change in wage inequality during the 1980s. For example, debate continues about the relative importance of institutional factors (like the decline in union contract coverage) and market forces (like technological change and increased international competition) in accounting for changes in the wage structure.

This study takes a substantially different perspective on the problem from that prevailing in the literature. It differs in three ways. First, it focuses on changes in the wage structure in a sample of local labor markets. Although the relevant labor market is local for most workers (at least in the short run) and although during the 1980s there were marked regional differences in economic performance, most earlier studies have looked at the national labor market.

Second, it examines changes in the structure of the wages paid for specific jobs. Most studies have used micro data from the Current Population Survey (CPS), which records the wages and salaries reported by individual workers. In the CPS data, however, it is difficult to sep-

1

arate the wage effects of labor-supply decisions about the hours of work, or multiple job-holding, or the wage effects of overtime pay, bonuses, and other wage supplements, from the wage paid for an hour of labor. This study uses data drawn from the Area Wage Surveys, which reported the distribution of wages paid by establishments for a number of job titles in a local labor market.

Third, it focuses on jobs and the skills required as the primary determinants of wages. The approach complements the more traditional human capital wage model, which emphasizes the personal characteristics of workers (Groshen 1996). One important aspect of the rise in wage inequality appears to be a coincident rise in the wage advantage accruing to highly skilled workers. Focusing on jobs allows us to examine the rise in the wage advantage by using data on several required skills that are more related to job performance than are schooling and potential experience, the two variables at the heart of the human capital approach.

By studying changes in the distribution of wages for specific jobs in a sample of local labor markets, we may find answers to the following questions:

1) Are trends in the structure of wages in local labor markets similar to the trends in the structure of wages revealed in nationwide studies?

2) Do local labor markets differ in the extent and pattern of the rise in wage inequality?

3) Have changes in the availability of benefits accompanied changes in the wage structure?

4) How have the wage returns on skills changed?

5) What is the relative importance of changes in union contract coverage and in the minimum wage in explaining changes in the wage structure?

WHAT DO WE KNOW?

The following brief summary of the literature on the rise in wage inequality during the 1980s seeks not to offer critiques, but rather to catalogue what is known about the rise in wage inequality and to identify issues that need further attention. A convenient starting point is the careful review of the literature by Levy and Murnane (1992).

Levy and Murnane identified several points about the rise in wage inequality during the 1980s. Among the more significant of these are the following:

1) For both men and women, the rise in wage inequality appears to have been driven largely by variation in wages, not by variation in the hours worked.

2) The rise in wage inequality, coupled with stagnant growth in real median wages, has resulted in a "hollowing out" of the middle range of the wage distribution.

3) Wage inequality between age groups and between groups with different levels of education was stable in the 1970s and rose sharply in the 1980s.

4) Wage inequality among workers of the same age and sex and with the same education has risen steadily since 1970.

5) Despite the considerable attention paid to de-industrialization, shifts of workers across industries and across occupations account for only a small portion of the rise in wage inequality during the 1980s.

In accounting for the rise in wage inequality overall, Levy and Murnane emphasized the importance of increases in inequality between and within groups stratified by skill level. Their analysis of wage inequality between groups points to a sharp rise in the wage advantage of more-educated, more-experienced, and generally more-skilled workers as the primary cause of greater inequality between groups. In turn, they traced the rise in skill advantage to a steady rise in the demand for skilled workers, perhaps due to technological change. Additionally, there is the hypothesis that greater international competition during the 1980s eroded the demand for less-skilled workers, even as increased immigration added to the supply. Levy and Murnane concluded that such supply-and-demand explanations of rising wage differences were generally consistent with much of the data available at the time of their review.

In their review of the literature on the causes of wage inequality within a group, however, Levy and Murnane found less convincing evidence in support of any one theory. While some researchers point to increasing returns on unmeasured skills in conjunction with rising returns on schooling as a possible explanation for rising wage inequality within a group, attempts to add extra skill measures to the basic human capital model did not strengthen the model's power. The evidence on widening plant-level wage differentials looks like a more promising avenue to explore. However, Levy and Murnane concluded their review by listing the growth of inequality within a group as an important piece of the puzzle.

A number of studies have been published since Levy and Murnane's review. The sections that follow summarize the contributions of those studies.

Returns on Skills

Almost all studies of changes in the relative wages of workers with different levels of education or experience find evidence of increases in the wage returns on higher labor market skills (for example, Buchinsky 1994; Card and Lemieux 1996). Differences in the returns on education have been found to play a big role in explaining international differences in the trend toward greater wage inequality (Gottschalk and Smeeding 1997). Wage inequality increased more in the United States and the United Kingdom than in Holland during the 1980s. In the United States and United Kingdom, a rising demand for workers with more education outstripped increases in the supply and drove up the relative wage for college-educated workers. In Holland, however, the supply of college-educated workers rose more rapidly than did the demand, and the college wage advantage in that country fell during the 1980s. These different patterns of change in the market for college-educated workers were significantly related to differences in trends in wage inequality for the three countries.

Additional Skill Variables

One problem with many studies of the returns on skill is that skill is measured solely by education and potential labor market experience. It's clear that the range of potentially relevant skills goes well beyond those two characteristics. This has led some labor economists to examine the wage effect of additional measures of skill to see whether evidence exists for a general increase in returns on skill and to identify worker traits that might help explain why wage inequality has risen for those with a given level of education.

Grogger and Eide (1995) examined the role of skills acquired prior to entering college and the role of the specific skills associated with various college majors to see the effects of each on the relative earnings of workers with different levels of college education. Skills learned prior to college were measured by high school grades and by performance on standardized tests. Data were taken from the National Longitudinal Study of the High School Class of 1972 and from the High School and Beyond Survey of high school graduates in 1980. Grogger and Eide found that mathematics ability, as measured by standardized test scores prior to college entry, had a statistically significant effect on workers' earnings, especially for women, and that the inclusion of that measure substantially eliminated any signs of an increased return on further education for women, but not for men, in the two high school classes. They also found that changes in the distribution of men across college majors during the 1980s tended toward highly skilled fields of study and helped to account for about 25 percent of the men's higher returns on additional years of college in the 1980 cohort.

Murnane, Willett, and Levy (1995) used the same data as Grogger and Eide to examine the effect of mathematics ability on workers' wages six years after high school graduation. An individual's score on the standardized mathematics test had a statistically significant positive relationship with wages. A comparison of the classes of 1972 and 1980 showed higher returns on schooling and on mathematics skill for men. For women, however, only the wage return on mathematics skill was higher for the class of 1980. Both classes had similar estimated wage returns on schooling. These two studies suggest that estimates of a rising college wage advantage may partially reflect changes over time in the composition of college students, by math ability and by major.

Constantine and Neumark (1996) added data on job training to a basic human capital model estimated separately for 1983 and 1991 CPS samples. As expected, more training was positively related to higher wages. However, they reported no evidence that the wage returns on training were higher in 1991 than in 1983, and the inclusion of training variables in the model had little impact on the finding that the estimated wage returns on schooling were higher in the 1991 sample.

The results of the three studies suggest that changes in the returns on skills are more complex than suggested by the estimates of the returns on schooling and potential experience found in the basic human capital model.[2] Individual cognitive skills, the skill content of the schooling chosen, and the amount of training received are all important determinants of the wage distribution. The results of the three studies also seem to confirm Levy and Murnane's conclusion that the skill measures generally available in data sets like the CPS are too broad to adequately test hypotheses about the rising demand for skilled workers during the 1980s.

Wage Instability

A difficulty with basing inferences about the wage structure on what workers report in earnings surveys such as the CPS is that changes in the earnings distribution can reflect changes in the economic situation of individual workers as well as changes in the wages for a given set of jobs. The severity of the recessions of the early 1980s and the prevalence of "downsizing," even during the economic recoveries of the late 1980s and 1990s, suggests that increased worker turnover and job turnover in a turbulent labor market might be an important factor contributing to increases in measured wage inequality.

Studies by Gottschalk and Moffitt (1994) and Gittleman and Joyce (1996) examined changes in the variance in wages over time in matched samples of workers. They decomposed the variance into permanent and transitory components, where the permanent component (the variance of individual earnings averaged over a number of years) is meant to capture changes in the wage structure. Both studies found that the increase in wage inequality during the 1980s reflected roughly equal increases in the variances of both the permanent and the transitory components of wages. In addition, Haveman and Buron (1994) concluded that changes in the utilization of earnings capacity may have played a more important role in accounting for increased wage inequality than is commonly thought. This suggests that special care must be taken to separate the sources of transitory wage instability from factors associated with fundamental changes in the wage distribution.

International Trade

Because the rise in wage inequality in the 1980s coincided with a period of sharp increases in the U.S. trade deficit, it is tempting to probe for links between the two. The examination of the effects of trade on the domestic wage distribution has generated considerable interest and debate. In part this reflects the anti-free-trade position of many who blame imports for deindustrialization and the hollowing out of the U.S. wage distribution.

Wood (1995) has been a strong proponent of the view that the opening of trade with less-developed countries during the 1980s had a large effect on the relative wage of skilled versus unskilled workers. Trade with less developed countries is seen as effectively raising the supply of less-skilled laborers in developed countries and as lowering their relative wage. Wood's factor-content analyses of trade generated support for that hypothesis. Several other studies have examined the impact of trade on the wage differential favoring the skilled.

For example, Borjas and Ramey (1995) identified a positive co-integrating relationship between the college/high school wage differential and the durable-goods trade deficit during the 1980s. By way of contrast, they did not find evidence that the college wage advantage was co-integrated with changes in the labor supply, unionization, research and development spending, or the nondurable goods trade deficit. Buckberg and Thomas (1996) also used the co-integration approach to find statistical evidence for a common movement over time in the college/high school wage differential and in changes in employment in durable goods manufacturing. They argued that changes in the number of jobs in that sector during the 1980s were highly sensitive to foreign trade.[3] Feenstra and Hanson (1996) found that both outsourcing (which they defined as the purchase of imported intermediate products) and import competition in final-goods markets are important in explaining changes in the wages of nonproduction workers relative to those of production workers across manufacturing industries between 1979 and 1990.[4]

Two other studies on the effects of trade relied on regional data for panel estimates of the effect on wage inequality. Borjas and Ramey (1995) found that the fraction of local employment in trade-affected concentrated industries was positively related to the college/high school wage differential in a sample of over 40 metropolitan areas in 1976 and 1990. They also calculated that the drop in employment in the subject industries during the period can explain as much as 14 percent of the rise in the college wage differential observed in their sample. Karoly and Klerman (1994) estimated the effect of durable goods imports relative to GNP in a model explaining the variance of the logarithm of real wages in a sample of 20 state and multistate regions from 1973 to 1988.[5] Their results, which controlled for unemployment, unionization, industry structure, age distribution, and regional fixed effects, showed that the import ratio had an important positive relationship with the variance of wages.

However, Karoly and Klerman worried that the correlation might be spurious because their trade measure varied only over time and the wage variance itself had a negative trend. Indeed, the problem of basing inferences of causality on the strongly trended time-series data led Sachs and Shatz (1996, p. 239) to conclude, "There is still no convincing quantitative account of the role of trade in the widening wage inequality, though theory and circumstantial evidence certainly support the linkage of trade and widening inequalities."

The main argument against international trade as a major determinant of rising wage inequality is that the percentage of U.S. employment accounted for by trade-affected manufacturing industries is too small to matter for the economy-wide changes in the wage structure during the 1980s (Burtless 1995). Topel (1997) pointed out that because the drop in the relative wage of unskilled workers has not been accompanied by a greater quantity demanded for them, factors other than a trade-induced increase in the supply of unskilled labor must be at work. Borjas, Freeman, and Katz (1997) undertook a careful analysis of the potential impact of both immigration and international trade on the relative earnings differentials associated with differences in education. They found that trade with developed countries has had no effect on the relative supply of unskilled workers and that the supply effect of trade with less-developed countries is quite modest, even given different assumptions about the domestic adjustment to trade. Neither trade nor immigration seems to explain much about the rise in the college wage advantage after 1980. Immigration did appear to be significant in explaining the precipitous drop in the relative earnings of high school dropouts during the 1980s.

A final piece of evidence on the impact of trade on the U.S. wage structure can be gleaned by comparing changes in wages in developed and less-developed countries. If comparative advantage is related to endowments of skilled and unskilled labor, factor-price equalization should work to raise the relative wages of less-skilled workers in less-developed countries while lowering those wages in developed countries. Interestingly, an examination of labor market developments in the United States, Canada, and Mexico after the signing of the North American Free Trade Agreement (NAFTA) reveals few differences. In particular, wage inequality trends in Mexico appear to have paralleled those in the United States. The Commission for Labor Cooperation (1997) reported the following Gini coefficients for the post-tax and post-transfer distribution of household income in Mexico: 0.43 in 1984, 0.47 in 1989, and 0.48 in 1994. Comparable figures for the United States are 0.40 in 1984, 0.42 in 1989, and 0.43 in 1994. The similarities add weight to Topel's (1997) contention that factor-price equalization has not been an important feature of recent wage structure changes in developed countries.

Technological Change

Some researchers have argued that we have only circumstantial evidence and theoretical support for arguing that technological change affects the wage distribution (Bound 1996). The issue is compounded by the difficulty of measuring technological change[6] and by the case-study evidence that new technology often results in the de-skilling of the workforce (Head 1996). Many economists, however, believe that technological change is the most logical explanation for the rise over time in both the wage advantage for workers with more education and skills and the relative use of skilled workers by U.S. businesses.

Some direct evidence on the issue comes from studies by Berman, Bound, and Griliches (1994) and by Machin, Ryan, and Van Reenan (1996) on the determinants of changes in the relative wages of non-production workers across manufacturing industries in the United States and the United Kingdom. Both studies reported that this gross measure of change in the skill differential was closely correlated with technological change (as measured by changes in capital, research and development, and computer intensity) across manufacturing industries and over time.

Krueger (1993) provided evidence on the wage effect of computer use on the job. He found that workers who used computers at work enjoyed wage levels in 1984 that were 18.5 percent higher than would have been predicted by a human capital model. Krueger also found that the wage advantage associated with computer use rose to 20.6 percent by 1989. Added evidence for a positive relationship between computer use and the demand for more highly skilled workers came from Autor, Katz, and Krueger (1997). Because much of the increase in technology during the 1980s can be associated with the acquisition of new computers and software by business firms, these results are taken as evidence that technological change has added to the demand for workers whose skills are suited to using the new technologies.

Other studies, however, question the importance of technological change in explaining the rise in wage inequality in the 1980s. Mishel and Bernstein (1996) examined the relationship between the skills demanded and the technology used across industries and compared the 1980s with the 1970s. They measured the mix of skills by the share of industry workers in fixed wage ranges and measured technological change by the computers and other equipment per worker and the share of scientists and engineers in the industry's workforce. Mishel and Bernstein found that the pace of technological change slowed during the 1980s and that, relative to the 1970s, technological change appeared to be less adverse for the bottom half of the wage distribution and less favorable for the highest-paid quartile in the 1980s. They also found that the employment share of workers in the quartile just above the median fell during the 1980s in the industries with the most rapid technological change.

Along with the argument that the timing of the most rapid technological change was incongruent with that of the fastest rise in wage inequality (Gottschalk and Smeeding 1997), other evidence also contradicts the findings of Berman, Bound, and Griliches (1994). Cappelli (1996) studied data from the 1984 EQW (National Center on the Educational Quality of the Workforce) National Employers Survey, which included measures of organizational technological change and data on the intensity of capital and computer use at the establishment level. He found that the ratio of the annual pay of production workers to that of supervisors was positively correlated with having a total quality management (TQM) program, with capital intensity, with the percentage of supervisors using computers, and with rising skill standards for production jobs. As with the attempts to quantify the trade-inequality relationship, the data may not permit an examination of what appears to be a highly complex relationship between technological change and changes in the structure of wages.

Skill Upgrading

As indicated, the rise in wage advantage associated with skilled work has been accompanied by a rise in the skill mix of the U.S. workforce. Employers are hiring relatively more skilled workers today than they did in the past, even though the labor market forces them to pay a significantly higher wage to skilled workers, which suggests the importance of shifts in labor demand.[7] While it seems obvious that such change in the skill mix of jobs would be related to technological change, the evidence yields mixed results. As with the evidence on the relationship between technology and wage inequality, the combined effect of a highly complex relationship between the skill mix and technological change and limited data for measuring technological change restricts our ability to measure the impact of technological change on skill upgrading.

For example, Howell and Wolff (1991 and 1992) and Wolff (1995) showed that differences in the pace of skill upgrading across industries were closely correlated with differences in capital intensity, computer use, and investment in research and development. The two studies also suggest that skill upgrading was most pronounced during the 1970s and may have slowed significantly during the rise in wage inequality in the 1980s.

Cappelli (1993, 1996) found some evidence that skill upgrading was correlated with the adoption of new office technology and with the introduction of total quality management and just-in-time production in manufacturing firms. However, he also found that significant skill downgrading occurred as a result of technological change in the computer support, office equipment, and telephone operator job categories. Head (1996) also cited many examples of skill downgrading in response to new technology, and Levy and Murnane's (1996) study of the introduction of computers in a bank department suggested that the changes in labor demand stemmed more from changes in the demand for the service than from changes in the skills required.

Institutions

Another group of studies focused on the role played by trade unions and by the minimum wage in the widening of wage inequality. During the 1980s, the relative drop in union membership, evident since the early 1960s, accelerated significantly. By the end of the decade, fewer than 20 percent of U.S. workers were covered by union contracts. Since unions have been found to have an equalizing effect on the wage distribution, the drop in union contract coverage has been seen as a possible cause of the widening wage gap. Indeed, Freeman (1993) calculated that the drop in union membership might account for as much as 40 percent of the rise in the college/high school wage differential in the United States. Machin (1997) estimated that the drop in union membership explained 40 percent of the 1983–1991 rise in the variance of the logarithm of annual wages in the United Kingdom. Karoly and Klerman's (1994) study of cross-state data for 1973–1988 found that falling rates of unionization led to higher variance in real wages. Freeman (1996) has argued that differences in collective bargaining institutions are the best explanation for the sharp differences in wage inequality between countries. Since Karoly and Klerman's study is the only one to estimate the effect of unions while controlling for other determinants of the variance in wages, it is not clear how robust these estimates are (Gottschalk and Smeeding 1997).

In the United States, the legal minimum wage also fell considerably in inflation-adjusted terms during the rise in wage inequality of the 1980s. Since the minimum wage establishes a legal floor for the wage distribution, the drop in its real value should have led to greater inequality, at least at the low-wage end of the distribution. Simulations by Horrigan and Mincy (1993) showed that keeping the real minimum wage constant during the 1980s would have had only modest effects on wage inequality among men. On the other hand, DiNardo, Fortin, and Lemieux (1996) estimated that the drop in the real minimum wage might account for 25 percent of the 1979–1988 rise in wage inequality among men and close to 30 percent of the rise in wage inequality among women. DiNardo and Lemieux (1997) noted that differences between the United States and Canada in both the drop in union membership and the fall in the minimum wage can account for two-thirds of the difference between those countries in the rise in wage inequality between 1981 and 1988. The relative importance of changes in unionization and in the minimum wage as determinants of growing wage inequality remains an important question for further study.

Race and Sex

The composition of the U.S. workforce by race and sex has changed substantially over time. From 1970 to 1997, the percentage of women in civilian employment rose from 38 percent to 46 percent, while the percentage of nonwhites rose from 11 percent to 15 percent. These changes could be expected to have augmented the rise in wage inequality since the wage level of both the median female and the median nonwhite worker falls well below the median for white males. And, to the extent that male/female and white/nonwhite wage ratios reflect skill differences, the strong rise in returns on skills would be expected to widen the wage gap for women and nonwhites.

In fact, those possibilities did not materialize. Schweitzer (1997) concluded that the importance of race and sex differentials in overall wage inequality dropped significantly from 1973 to 1991. Moreover, the trend toward rising overall wage inequality was accompanied by a drop in the male/female wage differential in both the United States (Blau and Kahn 1994) and the United Kingdom (Blackaby et al. 1997). There is also evidence of a stable racial wage differential in the United States during the 1980s (Card and Lemieux 1994).

The change in the demographic composition of the workforce has been accompanied by a rise in the relative experience and occupational standing of women and nonwhites. Blau and Kahn (1994) also found that the unexplained portion of the male/female wage differential has diminished over time. They attributed that to the combined effect of increased relative unmeasured skills, reduced labor market discrimination, and a shift in labor demand to patterns favoring women, especially those with lower skill levels. Thus the much-studied demographic differences in the U.S. labor market have not proven to be important in explaining the changes in the overall distribution of wages.

Within-Group Inequality

The increase in wage inequality in the United States and other countries has resulted both from changes in the relative wages across skill groups and from changes in the distribution of wages among workers with a given skill. In parallel with the evidence for rising wage returns on schooling, experience, and other measured forms of worker skill, the evidence for rising within-group inequality has been interpreted by Juhn, Murphy, and Pierce (1993) and others as the result of rising returns on unmeasured skills. Two recent studies looked at changes in wage inequality for specific occupational groups.

Ferrall's (1995) study of the rise in wage inequality among engineers from the mid 1970s to the mid 1980s found that it was largely explained by a rise in the wage differentials associated with higher levels of supervisory responsibility within firms. The rise was further traced to a shift in the demand, away from mid-career, middle-level engineers toward both younger, low-wage and older, higher-wage engineers.[8] This twist in the demand for engineers by skill level (which might reflect corporate downsizing) reveals more complexity in changing returns on skill than that seen in the evidence for schooling or for overall experience.

Baker, Gibbs, and Holmstrom (1994) examined the pay structure for managers in a single firm from 1969 to 1988. They identified three sources of inequality within that group. First, the mean real starting salary for cohorts of new managers was sensitive to the business cycle, falling markedly from 1974 to 1976, from 1979 to 1980, and from 1981 to 1982. This is important because differences in the mean salaries of different cohorts were highly correlated with differences in starting salaries. Second, individual real-wage levels within each cohort diverged significantly with tenure, reflecting rapid real-wage increases for high performance and promotions and the lack of real-wage protection for poor performers. Third, they noted that wage variances within all cohorts began to rise at a faster rate after 1980.

These papers illustrate how changing wage relationships within groups of homogenous workers can give rise to rising wage inequality. They also support the findings of Davis and Haltiwanger (1991) and Groshen (1991a, 1991b) that changes in the wage distribution within plants and firms can account for a substantial portion of changes in the wage structure for all workers.

THE SAMPLE OF LOCAL LABOR MARKETS

Our approach to the study of changes in wage inequality in local labor markets, much like the study by Karoly and Klerman (1994) already discussed, uses data for a panel of local labor markets tracked from 1974 to 1991. Substantial changes in the boundaries for an urban area often make it difficult to compare data over time. For that reason, the primary criterion used to select the areas for the sample was that the Area Wage Survey (AWS) boundaries be substantially unaltered for the period under study. The sample is also restricted to large urban areas because these had more extensive occupational coverage in the AWS and are more frequently included in other data sources, such as the *Geographic Profile of Employment and Unemployment*, than are smaller metropolitan areas.

Using these criteria, there are 20 large urban labor markets in the sample. These include the following 13 urban areas which had unchanged AWS boundaries: Anaheim, Chicago, Cincinnati, Cleveland, Indianapolis, Los Angeles, Miami, Milwaukee, Nassau–Suffolk, Philadelphia, San Diego, San Jose, and Seattle. The sample also includes five metropolitan labor markets which added one or more counties during the period studied but where the added counties accounted for 5 percent or less of the area's population in 1990. These are Atlanta, Baltimore, Detroit, Minneapolis, and St. Louis. Finally, the sample includes Houston and New York, even though their AWS boundaries were altered by the deletion of one county during the period. In each case, the population of the deleted county amounted to less than 10 percent of the area's 1990 population. The 20 areas then constitute the inter-urban, cross-section part of the data panel.

The time-series part of the panel reflects the fact that the AWS program consisted of two different employer surveys. About every third or fourth year, employers were visited by U.S. Bureau of Labor Statistics field agents who collected information on benefits and union contract coverage along with detailed occupational wage data. In the years between those employer visits, the Bureau used telephone and mail surveys to collect just the wage information. Since the interest here is in gradual structural changes, and since benefit and unionization data are of interest, the panel data set includes data only for the years in which Bureau field agents visited employers. The analysis begins with 1974, because a number of changes in the AWS methodology began in 1973, and it ends in 1991, because in that year the substantially altered Occupational Compensation Survey supplanted the Area Wage Survey. Table 1.1 lists the years in the time series for each of the 20 metropolitan labor markets. The unbalanced panel that results has 111 observations, with data from each year from 1974 to 1991 across the 20 metropolitan labor markets. (See Appendix A for details.)

Table 1.1 Metropolitan Areas and Survey Years in the Panel Data Set

Metropolitan area	Years					
Anaheim	1975	1978	1981	1984	1988	
Atlanta	1975	1978	1981	1984	1987	1991
Baltimore	1975	1978	1981	1984	1987	1991
Chicago	1974	1977	1980	1983	1986	
Cincinnati	1974	1977	1979	1982	1985	1989
Cleveland	1974	1977	1980	1983	1986	1990
Detroit		1976	1979	1982	1985	1989
Houston	1974	1977	1980	1983	1986	1990
Indianapolis	1975	1978	1981	1984	1988	
Los Angeles	1975	1978	1981	1984	1986	1989
Miami	1975	1978	1981	1984	1987	1990
Milwaukee	1975	1978	1981	1984	1987	1991
Minneapolis	1975	1978	1981	1984	1987	1991
Nassau–Suffolk	1975	1978	1981	1984	1987	
New York	1975	1978	1981	1985	1989	
Philadelphia	1976	1979	1982	1985	1988	
St. Louis	1976	1979	1982	1985	1989	
San Diego	1974	1977	1980	1983	1986	1989
San Jose	1975	1978	1981	1984	1988	
Seattle	1974	1977	1979	1982	1985	1988

The local labor markets in the sample are fairly well dispersed around the country. Three areas are in the Northeast census division, eight are in the Midwest division, four are in the South, and five in the West. The 20 areas in the sample are also fairly well dispersed in terms of the economic performance of their manufacturing sectors during the 1980s. A recent study by Noponen, Markusen, and Driessen (1997) provides a shift-share analysis of changes in employment in U.S. Metropolitan Statistical Areas (MSAs) from 1978 to 1986 and gives measures of the sensitivity of the local mix of manufacturing to exports, imports, and productivity growth. Their cluster analysis of the data led them to a fourfold classification of metropolitan areas. They identify "trade winners" as MSAs with a manufacturing mix that generated strong performance in domestic and export markets and saw high growth in productivity. The trade winners included Anaheim, Minneapolis, Nassau–Suffolk, San Diego, and San Jose, all in the sample of local labor markets.

Four areas in the sample fall into Noponen, Markusen, and Driessen's "trade loser" category, areas where the manufacturing mix exhibited weak domestic and export performance. The four areas are Cleveland, Detroit, Houston, and Milwaukee. Five areas from the sample—Indianapolis, Los Angeles, New York, Philadelphia and Seattle—are included in the strong domestic market category of their study. The remaining areas in the sample—Atlanta, Chicago, Cincinnati, Miami, and St. Louis—are identified as MSAs having import-resistant industry mixes. The sample of 20 local labor markets is evenly spread among their four categories of metropolitan area manufacturing performance. The categories are not, however, closely related to the census divisions for the areas in our sample. One can find Rust-Belt and Sun-Belt areas in each of their four clusters.

THE AREA WAGE SURVEY DATA

The AWS program began in the late 1940s and collected information on wages and benefits for jobs common to a wide range of industries where local economic conditions were important determinants of pay.[9] Over the years, the AWS expanded to cover more job titles and more places. In 1991, it was replaced by the Occupational Compensation Survey. The AWS covered firms in six private-sector industries: 1) manufacturing, 2) transportation, communication and public utilities, 3) wholesale trade, 4) retail trade, 5) finance, insurance, and real estate, and 6) services. Small firms, generally those with fewer than 50 employees, were excluded from the surveys. The site visits sampled firms by industry and by number of employees. In reports of combined data, firms were weighted according to their probability of selection in order to generate unbiased estimates.

The job titles included in the AWS were grouped into four occupations: 1) office-clerical workers, 2) professional and technical employees, 3) maintenance, toolroom, and power-plant workers, and 4) material movement and custodial workers. For brevity, this study refers to the four occupational groups as the office-clerical, professional-technical, skilled maintenance, and material movement groups. Table 1.2 lists the job titles included in each occupational group. Although workers in just 41 job titles are included in the data for the study, those job titles represent a substantial portion of the total employment in firms surveyed in the AWS. For example, in the December 1989 Area Wage Survey for Los Angeles, the total number of workers in those job titles was 172,096. That represented almost

Table 1.2   Job Titles for the Four Area Wage Survey Occupation Groups

Office-Clerical	Skilled Maintenance
Secretary	Carpenter
Stenographer	Electrician
Typist	Painter
Word processor	Machinist
Key entry operator	Maintenance mechanic
Accounting clerk	Pipefitter
Payroll clerk	Millwright
File clerk	Motor vehicle mechanic
Messenger	General maintenance worker
Receptionist	Machine-tool operator
Switchboard operator	Tool and die maker
	Stationary engineer

Professional-Technical	Material Movement
Computer systems analyst	Truck driver
Computer programmer	Shipper and receiver
Computer operator	Warehouseman
Drafter	Order filler
Electronics technician	Shipping packer
Registered industrial nurse	Material handling laborer
	Forklift operator
	Guard
	Janitor

one-third of Los Angeles' 521,813 workers, which included executives, managers, full-time production and office workers, and seasonal and part-time workers employed in the surveyed establishments. There is also evidence that wages for those jobs are representative of wages in closely related jobs that were not covered by the AWS (Special Reports Group 1975).

The AWS allocated job titles through a uniform set of job descriptions designed to account for inter-firm differences in duties. The AWS also collected wage data for full-time workers who worked a regular weekly schedule. The data excluded overtime pay; weekend, holiday, and late-shift premiums; and bonuses and lump-sum payments. It reported regular straight-time weekly salaries and standard workweek hours for the office-clerical and professional-technical groups, so it is possible to estimate hourly wage rates for workers in those jobs.

The AWS data offer some advantages for studying changes in the wage structure in local labor markets. One important advantage is that the AWS collected data on-site on the wages for full-time workers in specific jobs. Thus there is less need for concern about the potential impact of job turnover or of errors in worker-reported earnings (Gottschalk and Moffitt 1994). A second advantage is that the AWS data covered large numbers of workers drawn from stratified samples representative of medium and large firms in specific industries in each locality. While the CPS could be used to construct local-area samples, its sample sizes for each area are small, and the survey itself is designed to be nationally, not locally, representative.

The main disadvantage of the AWS data is that it did not include information on workers' personal characteristics or on the characteristics of their employers. While the AWS data precludes estimating a human capital model, there is a growing recognition that job-related wage determinants, such as the occupation or the size of the firm, add substantially to the usefulness of the human capital model (Groshen 1996). The sample here uses job-skill requirements from the *Dictionary of Occupational Titles* to examine the effects of skill on wages. Groshen (1996) noted that since the AWS program covered workers in jobs common to a wide variety of employers, the AWS wage data may be less affected by employer-specific wage determinants than would be the case for jobs that are found only in a limited range of firms and industries.

THE PLAN OF THIS BOOK

Chapters 2 and 3 present a descriptive analysis of changes over time in the structure of wages in the panel of 20 metropolitan labor markets. Chapter 2 concentrates on trends in the variance of the logarithm of real hourly wage rates and on trends in the real wage differentials between the 75th and 50th percentiles and the 50th and 25th percentiles of the wage distribution. In general, Chapter 2 concludes that changes in the local wage structure over time follow patterns similar to those found in earlier studies of national data. Chapter 3 looks at trends in the availability of benefits (for example, health insurance and pensions) and at the extent of union contract coverage across the 20 labor markets over time. Changes in benefit coverage were not as extensive as changes in wage rates and appear to have been closely related to union contract coverage.

Chapters 4 and 5 examine determinants of the level and distribution of wages. Chapter 4 tests the hypothesis that returns on skills rose during the 1980s. It uses regressions for the average real hourly wages for specific job titles and for the measures of skills required for those jobs, comparing results for the late 1970s with those for the late 1980s. While evidence exists for a general rise in returns on skills, the results vary considerably for training, job level, cognitive skills, and machine-related skills. Chapter 5 examines the role of labor market forces, union contract coverage, and the real minimum wage in explaining the changes in wage structure. The results suggest that changes in wage inequality both between and within occupational groups were closely related to all three variables. The study ends with a summary chapter that examines some policy implications of the research.

Notes

1. Throughout this text, *wage inequality* means the degree to which hourly wage rates are unequally distributed among individual workers. *Wage dispersion* is a synonym for wage inequality. *Wage structure* refers to the way hourly wages vary among workers due to their occupation, industry, skill level, etc. Changes in the wage structure are an important cause of increased wage inequality.
2. Cognitive skills reflect a person's ability in language, mathematics, reasoning, and problem solving. While cognitive skills are related to years of schooling,

they also vary considerably among individuals having a given level of educational attainment.

3. However, an interesting analysis by McConnell and Quiros (1998) reported a statistically significant reduction in the volatility of U.S. real GDP growth after 1984. They traced this to a reduced volatility in the production of durable consumer goods associated with a decline in the inventory ratio in the industry.

4. Bernard and Jensen (1997) also found that changes in the relative wages and employment of nonproduction workers in U.S. manufacturing were affected by trade. In their study, however, export sales rather than import competition proved to be important.

5. Throughout this book, the use of the term *logarithm* refers to natural logarithms.

6. While it might be expected that the labor market effects of trade are easier to measure than those related to technological change, considerable debate has emerged over the relevance of factor-content versus relative prices as a trade-impact variable and over the appropriate method of calculating the factor-content of trade. See Burtless (1995) and Wood (1995).

7. Gregg and Manning (1997) emphasized that in the long run the skill-supply response determines relative wages and employment. While the skill supply depends in part on incentives for workers investing in new skills, they argue that such decisions are also very responsive to public policy.

8. This pattern was also found by Gittleman and Howell (1995) in their study of shifts in employment across job clusters that were closely linked to skill requirements.

9. The description of the AWS survey program and its methods is based on Scofea (1986), Hotchkiss (1990), and Barkume (1996), and on the Scope and Method of Survey Appendix to the published AWS Reports. See also the *BLS Measures of Compensation* (Bureau of Labor Statistics 1986).

2 Trends in the Urban Wage Structure

In this chapter, I use data drawn from Area Wage Surveys to describe changes in the structure of wages in the sample of 20 urban labor markets from 1974 to 1991. I examine the wage structure in terms of the central tendency and degree of inequality in the local distribution of real hourly wages. Data on the median real hourly wage, the variance of the natural logarithm of the real hourly wage, and the difference between the logarithm of the real hourly wage at the 75th, 50th, and 25th percentiles of the wage distribution are used to describe changes in the wage structure. Before considering the extent to which changes in local wage structures can be contrasted with the national data discussed in Chapter 1, this chapter examines data on changes in the occupational mix of employment.

EMPLOYMENT TRENDS

Table 2.1 presents data on the total number of workers in the firms surveyed and on the distribution of workers among the four occupational groups for the initial and final years for each metropolitan area in the sample. Local labor markets are arranged in Table 2.1 by census division to facilitate regional comparisons. The first point to note about the data in Table 2.1 is that the sample sizes are relatively large. The smallest is the 16,107 workers covered by the 1974 AWS in San Diego.

A comparison of the samples for the initial and final years for each area reveals definite regional patterns. Between the mid 1970s and the end of the 1980s, 9 of the 11 areas in the Northeast and Midwest divisions showed a drop in the number of workers in firms covered by the AWS. Only Nassau–Suffolk and Indianapolis showed an increase in the number of workers covered. In contrast, with the exception of Baltimore, all areas in the South and West divisions showed an increase in the number of workers in firms surveyed by the AWS. The extent to which the changes represent changes in the sample design rather

Table 2.1 Sample Size and Occupational Distribution Changes

Metropolitan area/years		Sample size	Share of sample (%)			
			Office-clerical	Professional-technical	Skilled maintenance	Material movement
Northeast						
Nassau–Suffolk	1975	28,607	39.9	12.2	7.8	40.1
	1987	42,505	34.3	18.0	6.2	41.5
New York	1975	251,489	46.5	8.0	4.1	41.3
	1989	165,257	33.8	10.2	5.7	50.3
Philadelphia	1976	110,119	33.9	9.4	15.7	41.0
	1988	98,604	27.7	16.0	12.0	44.2
Midwest						
Chicago	1974	255,074	34.0	7.5	13.2	45.3
	1986	168,360	31.9	13.4	13.4	41.2
Cincinnati	1974	41,057	31.4	6.0	13.4	49.1
	1989	31,980	27.6	14.2	18.0	40.2
Cleveland	1974	61,526	31.2	8.4	19.0	4.4
	1990	34,295	25.1	16.5	20.4	37.9
Detroit	1976	129,888	23.9	9.0	24.0	43.0
	1989	93,524	19.9	16.5	23.5	40.1
Indianapolis	1975	34,979	31.7	7.2	16.8	44.3
	1988	29,764	29.3	15.1	17.0	38.5
Milwaukee	1975	39,699	31.1	9.7	17.8	41.4
	1991	39,883	23.2	17.8	15.6	43.4
Minneapolis	1975	70,221	35.1	11.0	8.6	45.3
	1991	51,329	32.6	21.7	8.6	37.0

St. Louis	1976	70,564	32.0	6.9	18.4	42.7
	1989	60,821	28.9	14.1	16.9	40.0
South						
Atlanta	1975	54,741	37.7	7.9	7.9	46.6
	1991	65,161	28.1	17.4	7.0	47.5
Baltimore	1975	55,645	26.8	8.7	12.4	52.0
	1991	40,034	22.3	13.5	8.8	55.2
Houston	1974	63,133	31.8	8.6	12.3	46.7
	1990	66,807	25.7	13.9	9.3	50.6
Miami	1975	31,215	35.1	6.9	5.5	52.5
	1990	36,715	33.6	10.3	6.3	49.3
West						
Anaheim	1975	26,735	38.0	13.9	7.3	40.3
	1988	39,865	37.7	16.8	7.9	37.5
Los Angeles	1975	162,823	40.1	9.4	8.5	42.0
	1989	172,096	30.5	10.8	7.8	50.8
San Diego	1974	16,107	41.7	19.4	7.4	31.5
	1989	29,630	30.0	15.4	6.0	48.6
San Jose	1975	22,539	35.5	22.5	11.4	30.5
	1988	38,573	33.2	27.0	3.5	36.5
Seattle	1974	26,243	41.7	12.9	10.0	35.4
	1988	32,004	32.7	17.0	8.0	42.2

SOURCE: Author's calculations from the Area Wage Surveys.

than changes in the number of jobs cannot be determined, but the patterns are consistent with the shift in economic activity from the older, industrial Northeast toward the Southwest during the period.

While there is considerable variation among localities in the occupational distribution of employment, in all cases the samples are more heavily weighted toward job titles in the office-clerical and material movement groups. Changes in the distribution generally match the conclusion, summarized in Chapter 1, that employers have shifted toward hiring more educated workers. That shift is clearly seen in the data for office-clerical and professional-technical jobs. In all 20 local labor markets, the percentage of workers in office-clerical jobs dropped over time, while in 19 of the 20, the percentage in professional-technical jobs rose. In Cincinnati, Indianapolis, Minneapolis, St. Louis, and Atlanta, the percentage in the mainly computer-oriented professional-technical jobs more than doubled. The five western metropolitan areas generally experienced the smallest shift toward professional-technical jobs.

Changes in the blue-collar mix were more complex than those for office-clerical and professional-technical workers. While the evidence shows a pronounced relative increase over time in the employment of skilled white-collar technical workers, the percentage of skilled maintenance workers fell in 12 areas, rose in 7, and remained unchanged in Minneapolis. Four of the seven areas that registered an increase in the percentage of skilled maintenance workers were in the Midwest, and the greatest drops were in the South and West.

The changes in the relative importance of material movement workers in AWS-surveyed firms varied widely across the four census divisions. The percentage employed in these jobs rose in the three areas in the Northeast, fell in seven of the eight areas in the Midwest, and rose in three of the four areas in the South and four of the five in the West. Job growth appears to have led to a relative increase in less-skilled blue-collar jobs relative to skilled maintenance jobs. The opposite shift appears to be the case for local labor markets where employment fell in establishments covered by the AWS.

MEDIAN REAL WAGE TRENDS

This study now turns to the trends in the median real hourly wage for workers in the 41 occupations in each of the 20 metropolitan areas.

Hourly wages for workers in the clerical and technical groups are computed by dividing the weekly wages by the weighted average of the usual weekly hours worked across the job titles for each occupation. Hourly wages are also deflated by the local consumer price index.[1] Because of the mix of occupations in the study, the Consumer Price Index for Urban Wage Earners and Clerical Workers (CPI-W) is used. Because there is no local CPI-W for Indianapolis, real hourly wages for that area are calculated by using the CPI-W for the North Central region, and because the Miami CPI-W begins in 1978, the CPI-W for the South is used to determine real wages in Miami for 1975. In all cases, the CPI-W for the month or semiannual period closest to the AWS survey month is used to deflate the wage data.

Table 2.2 presents data for the median real hourly wage for workers in the 20 local labor markets in the sample, grouped alphabetically by census division. For comparison, Table 2.2 also presents national data, drawn from the Current Population Survey (CPS), for the real median hourly wages and salaries for all wage and salary workers. The data from the CPS for 1975 to 1989 is taken from Karoly (1993).

The CPS real median wage follows a generally pro-cyclical pattern: rising by 1.2 percent from 1975 to 1978, falling by 4.05 percent during the recession of 1978 to 1982, and rising by 5.4 percent from 1982 to 1989. The rather slight 1.2 percent rate of increase in median real wages (as measured by the CPS) over the decade and a half after 1975 would appear to result from the significant drop in real wages during the severe recessions of the early 1980s, recessions which interrupted a span of rising real wages. Given the considerable effort by labor economists to measure the cyclical behavior of the aggregate real wage, it is of considerable note that a glance at the data is enough to suggest a distinctly pro-cyclical pattern, albeit one that is of markedly lower frequency in the time series than the typical business cycle indicators.

The generally pro-cyclical pattern—rising real wages in the late 1970s, falling real wages during the 1980 and 1981–1982 recessions, and rising real wages in the recovery—can also be seen in the AWS data for several local labor markets in the sample, even though the periodic nature of the local time-series data obscures annual wage changes. Almost all areas show a significant drop in the real median wage during the early 1980s. Only Seattle and Cincinnati, where the real median wage fell from 1977 to 1979 but rose from 1979 to 1982,

Table 2.2 Median Real Hourly Wage Rates, All Workers ($)

Metropolitan area	1974	1975	1976	1977	1978	1979	1980	1981	1982	1983	1984	1985	1986	1987	1988	1989	1990	1991
Northeast																		
Nassau–Suffolk		7.41			7.16			6.89			7.10			7.16				
New York		7.98			8.48			7.75				8.27				8.95		
Philadelphia			8.65			8.13			7.71			7.95			7.91			
Midwest																		
Chicago	8.66			9.13			8.41			8.39			8.98					
Cincinnati	8.43			8.96		7.97			8.11			8.60				8.30		
Cleveland	9.25			9.36			8.51			8.39			8.65				8.30	
Detroit			11.34			11.90			11.53			11.73				11.76		
Indianapolis		8.42			8.70			8.18			8.70				8.19			
Milwaukee		9.50			9.83			8.66			8.58			8.43				8.25
Minneapolis		8.96			9.07			7.94			8.61			8.60				8.54
St. Louis			9.48			8.99			8.19			8.56				8.44		
South																		
Atlanta		7.46			7.20			7.02			6.99			7.50				7.36
Baltimore		7.61			8.53			7.87			7.38			6.86				6.81
Houston	7.53			7.58			7.31			7.67			7.85					
Miami		6.80			6.65			6.25			6.35			6.09				
West																		
Anaheim		8.15			8.54			7.41			8.03				8.22			
Los Angeles		8.55			8.28			7.39			8.46		8.99				8.43		
San Diego	8.70			8.85			7.05			7.77			7.63				7.16	
San Jose					9.30			8.75			9.32				9.27			
Seattle	9.54	10.00		9.16		9.09			9.19			9.32			9.16			
U.S.A. (CPS data)	6.84	6.88		6.89	6.92	6.86	6.76	6.66	6.64	6.68	6.66	6.70	6.95	6.90	6.99	6.98		

SOURCE: The national data are from the Current Population Survey, reported by Karoly (1993). Local area data are from the Area Wage Surveys, author's calculations. See Appendix B for details on estimation techniques.

fail to follow the pattern. A look at the 11 areas with AWS data for 1978 and 1981 shows a negative rate of change in the real median wage between those two years for every area, a rate ranging from –4.6 percent for Nassau–Suffolk to –12.4 percent for Minneapolis. The recession-caused drop in real wages was not limited to the Rust Belt. Real median wages fell by 3.6 percent in Houston from 1977 to 1980, by 7.7 percent in Anaheim from 1978 to 1981, by 2.9 percent in Atlanta from 1977 to 1984, and by 6 percent in Miami from 1978 to 1981. Thus, both national (CPS) and local (AWS) data point to the recessions of the early 1980s as playing a very significant role in the changes in the real median wage since 1974.

Unlike the pattern in the CPS real median wage, the local (AWS) real median wage generally did not rise enough during the recovery of 1984 to 1989 to offset the effects of the recession of the 1980s. Every area but Anaheim, Chicago, Detroit, and New York saw lower real median wages at the end of the 1980s than in the mid 1970s. In Baltimore and Milwaukee, real median wages fell throughout the 1980s, even during the long expansion that began in 1984.

Evidence for a pro-cyclical movement in real median wages also appears in the eight labor markets with AWS data for 1990 or 1991. Real median wages fell from 1986 to 1990 in Cleveland, Houston, and San Diego, and from 1987 to 1990 or 1991 in Atlanta, Baltimore, Milwaukee, and Minneapolis. The 1990–1991 recession, exacerbated in Houston by a major decline in the oil industry after 1986, appears to have lowered median real wages for workers in the sample for those eight labor markets in a fashion similar to the downturns of 1980 and 1981–1982.

TRENDS IN WAGE INEQUALITY

While there are many metrics used to assess the characteristics of the distribution of wages, this study follows the recent literature and focuses on two. The variance of the logarithm of real hourly wages is used to measure the overall degree of wage inequality in each area and year in the sample. This study also looks at the extent to which changes in the wage inequality reflect differences in the relative wages between workers at the upper and lower reaches of that distribution.

It uses the differences between the logarithm of the real hourly wage of workers at the 75th and 50th percentiles and at the 50th and 25th percentiles in the analysis.

Table 2.3 presents data on the variance of the logarithm of the real hourly wage for each city/year observation. Unlike the patterns noted in the data for the median real wage, the variances reported in Table 2.3 show a steady rise for each local labor market. The only exception to that pattern is a slight drop for several areas at the end of the time series.

The increase in wage inequality is quite substantial. The mean of the annual rate of increase in the variance is 3.4 percent across the 20 areas. The annual rate of change in the variance, calculated from the initial to the final available year, is 4 percent or higher for Cleveland, Houston, Seattle, New York, San Jose, San Diego, Detroit, and St. Louis. As measured by the annual rate of change, the variance increased the least in Anaheim, Baltimore, and Nassau–Suffolk. While individual areas show obvious differences in the change in the variance, no broad regional patterns appear in the data of Table 2.3.

The variances based on the AWS data for workers in the 41 occupations in the sample are comparable, in magnitude and trend, to national data on workers in all occupations drawn from the Current Population Survey. Karoly and Klerman (1994) calculated the variance in the logarithm of the real wage for male workers from the May outgoing-rotation groups in the CPS. Their estimated variances for the nation and for ten of the most populous states (which include many of the areas in this study's sample) for 1973 and 1989 are shown in Table 2.4

Real hourly wages in this study's sample of local labor markets are slightly less dispersed about the mean than in the national and state data shown above. This undoubtedly reflects the much narrower range of occupations in the local data and also reflects the assumption that all workers are at the midpoint of reported wage cells in the AWS. Between 1973 and 1988, the annual rate of increase in the variance was 2.5 percent for the United States and averaged 3.11 percent for the 10 states. The latter rate falls just below the 3.4 percent average for the annual rate of change across the 20 areas studied here. The rise in the 1980s variance of the logarithm of real wages shown in Table 2.3 does not appear to be particular to the AWS data, but rather seems to parallel the findings from broader national samples.

Table 2.3 The Variance of the Logarithm of Real Hourly Wage Rates, All Workers

Metropolitan area	1974	1975	1976	1977	1978	1979	1980	1981	1982	1983	1984	1985	1986	1987	1988	1989	1990	1991	Annual rate of change (%)
Northeast																			
Nassau–Suffolk		0.1076			0.1334			0.1541			0.1641			0.1411					3.4
New York		0.0895			0.1089			0.1299				0.1716				0.1649			4.5
Philadelphia			0.1143			0.1544			0.1875			0.1825			0.1787				3.8
Midwest																			
Chicago	0.0975			0.1157			0.1330			0.1449			0.1550						3.9
Cincinnati	0.1205			0.1433		0.1464			0.1734			0.1965				0.1889			3.0
Cleveland	0.1163			0.1409			0.1451			0.1472			0.1880				0.2379		4.5
Detroit			0.1152			0.1005			0.1508			0.1702				0.1993			4.3
Indianapolis		0.1535			0.1731			0.1883			0.2104				0.2165				2.7
Milwaukee		0.1229			0.1450			0.1597			0.1897			0.2365				0.1907	2.8
Minneapolis		0.1167			0.1331			0.1432			0.1348			0.1636				0.1601	2.0
St. Louis			0.1356			0.1631			0.1848			0.2341				0.2370			4.1
South																			
Atlanta		0.1249			0.1717			0.1817			0.1904			0.1856				0.2003	3.0
Baltimore		0.1584			0.1784			0.2126			0.2336			0.2493				0.2024	1.5
Houston	0.1562			0.1755			0.1700			0.1881			0.2205				0.3113		4.4
Miami		0.1233			0.1300			0.1397			0.1596		0.2008				0.1821		2.6
West																			
Anaheim		0.1289			0.1347			0.1256			0.1499				0.1571				1.5
Los Angeles		0.1238			0.1342			0.1368			0.1485		0.1893				0.1808		2.6
San Diego				0.1270			0.1508			0.1924			0.2248			0.2001			4.0
San Jose		0.0899			0.1142			0.1148			0.1251				0.152				4.1
Seattle	0.0943			0.1230		0.1483			0.1504			0.1676			0.1718				4.4

SOURCE: Authors' calculations from the Area Wage Surveys. See Appendix B for details. The annual rate of change is calculated for the initial to the final year for each metropolitan area.

Table 2.4   Variance in ln(Real Wage) for Males

Location	1973	1989
United States	0.199	0.288
New York	0.176	0.289
Pennsylvania	0.164	0.261
Ohio	0.145	0.250
Indiana	0.152	0.244
Illinois	0.164	0.279
Michigan	0.164	0.268
Wisconsin	0.152	0.264
Florida	0.202	0.273
Texas	0.257	0.328
California	0.194	0.324

SOURCE: Karoly and Klerman (1994).

Table 2.5 presents data on trends in differences in the logarithm of the real hourly wage between workers at the 75th and 50th (75–50) percentiles and at the 50th and 25th (50–25) percentiles of the wage distribution for each city. For ease of presentation, Table 2.5 includes only data for the initial and final year for each area. For comparison, the last row of the table also includes the 1975 and 1989 75–50 and 50–25 wage gaps for all wage and salary workers in the national CPS data in Karoly (1993).

The indication from Table 2.5 is again one of a general widening of the wage gap in each labor market under study. The real wage gap between workers at the upper quartile and the median (the 75–50 differential) rose in 16 of the 20 areas. It is noteworthy that among the five areas without an increase in the 75–50 differential are the contiguous east coast MSAs of New York and Nassau–Suffolk and the contiguous west coast MSAs of Los Angeles and Anaheim. Relative wage trends in the local labor markets for highly paid workers in these very large conurbations appear to have been substantially different than those in most other areas and the country as a whole. However, the entries for the initial and final years in Table 2.5 for New York, Nassau–Suffolk, Los Angeles, Anaheim, and Minneapolis obscure the fact that the 75–50 wage differential in these areas first rose and then fell during the intervening years. There does not appear to be a distinct

Table 2.5   Percentile Wage Differentials, All Workers

Metropolitan area/years	75–50 Differential			50–25 Differential		
	Initial year	Final year	Annual rate of change (%)	Initial year	Final year	Annual rate of change (%)
Northeast						
Nassau–Suffolk 1975/1987	0.26	0.26	0	0.22	0.26	1.29
New York 1975/1989	0.19	0.17	−0.79	0.16	0.32	5.07
Philadelphia 1976/1988	0.28	0.30	0.57	0.27	0.37	2.66
Midwest						
Chicago 1974/1986	0.28	0.30	0.57	0.20	0.31	3.71
Cincinnati 1974/1989	0.23	0.27	1.07	0.25	0.33	1.87
Cleveland 1974/1990	0.24	0.38	2.91	0.28	0.41	2.41
Detroit 1976/1989	0.16	0.20	1.60	0.28	0.49	4.07
Indianapolis 1975/1988	0.32	0.41	1.92	0.33	0.35	0.45
Milwaukee 1975/1991	0.26	0.33	1.50	0.28	0.40	2.25
Minneapolis 1975/1991	0.28	0.27	−0.23	0.26	0.33	1.50
St. Louis 1976/1989	0.22	0.33	3.17	0.35	0.43	1.60
South						
Atlanta 1975/1991	0.28	0.36	1.58	0.22	0.33	2.56
Baltimore 1975/1991	0.32	0.38	1.08	0.33	0.37	0.72
Houston 1974/1990	0.31	0.46	2.49	0.30	0.62	4.64
Miami 1975/1990	0.24	0.30	1.50	0.24	0.27	0.78
West						
Anaheim 1975/1988	0.29	0.26	−0.84	0.21	0.27	1.95
Los Angeles 1975/1989	0.25	0.25	0	0.30	0.40	2.08
San Diego 1974/1989	0.21	0.35	3.46	0.24	0.45	4.27
San Jose 1975/1988	0.21	0.26	1.66	0.24	0.27	0.91
Seattle 1974/1988	0.25	0.35	2.43	0.27	0.31	0.99
National (CPS data) 1975/1939	0.41	0.45	0.67	0.45	0.48	0.46

SOURCE: Author's calculations from the Area Wage Surveys. National data are from Karoly (1993). The differentials measure the difference between the ln(real wage) at the 75th (50th) percentile minus the ln(real wage) at the 50th (25th) percentile.

regional pattern among those areas showing increases in the 75–50 wage gap. Large increases are seen for Cleveland and St. Louis in the Midwest, Houston in the South, and San Diego and Seattle in the West.

Table 2.5 also points to a substantial deterioration in the relative wage of workers in the lower quartile of the wage distribution. The 50–25 wage differential increased in all 20 urban areas and doubled in New York and Houston. In 13 areas, the increases in the 50–25 gap exceeded the rise in the 75–50 gap, suggesting that the rise in wage inequality in many areas was due more to a relative decrease at the lowest quartile than to a rise at the highest. That conclusion applies particularly to New York, Philadelphia, Chicago, Detroit, Houston, Anaheim, and Los Angeles. For Indianapolis, Seattle, and St. Louis, on the other hand, the rise in the 75–50 differential greatly exceeded the increase in the 50–25 differential. Cincinnati, Cleveland, Baltimore, San Diego, and San Jose showed a fairly symmetrical rise in inequality, with both wage gaps rising by approximately equal amounts. Symmetry is also seen in the national CPS data, although the increases in the local wage gaps are much larger than those in the CPS series.

VARIANCE DECOMPOSITION

A useful feature of the variance of the logarithm of the real wage as a measure of wage dispersion is the relative ease with which the variance can be decomposed into the variance within and the variance between groups. As shown in the following formula (Juhn, Murphy, and Pierce 1993), the overall variance in each year can be partitioned into the weighted average of the wage variance within each group and into the weighted average of the group relative wage differential:

Eq. 2.1 $$\sigma_t^2 = \sum_i p_{it}\, \sigma_{it}^2 + \sum_i p_{it}\, (W_{it} - W_t)^2$$

where p_{it} is the fraction of workers in group i for time period t, and W_{it} is the logarithm of the average wage of workers in group i for time t. Substantial evidence, summarized in Chapter 1, suggests that much of the rise in wage inequality took place within specific groups. In this study, the natural decomposition runs along the lines of the four major occupational groups in the AWS. In the variance decomposi-

Table 2.6   Variance Decomposition for All Occupational Groups

Metropolitan area/years		Variance Overall	Between-group	Within-group	Within-group (% of overall)	ΔWithin-group/ ΔOverall (%)
Northeast						
Nassau–	1975	0.1076	0.0262	0.0814	75.7	40.3
Suffolk	1987	0.1411	0.0462	0.0949	67.3	
New York	1975	0.0895	0.0206	0.0689	77.0	66.7
	1989	0.1649	0.0456	0.1192	72.3	
Philadelphia	1976	0.1143	0.0306	0.0837	73.2	71.3
	1988	0.1787	0.0491	0.1296	72.5	
Midwest						
Chicago	1974	0.0975	0.0287	0.0688	70.5	73.3
	1986	0.1550	0.0441	0.1109	71.5	
Cincinnati	1974	0.1205	0.0268	0.0937	77.8	49.1
	1989	0.1889	0.0616	0.1273	67.4	
Cleveland	1974	0.1163	0.0391	0.0772	66.4	40.4
	1990	0.2379	0.1115	0.1263	53.1	
Detroit	1976	0.1152	0.0412	0.0741	64.3	71.6
	1989	0.1993	0.0650	0.1342	67.4	
Indianapolis	1975	0.1535	0.0455	0.1079	70.3	63.3
	1988	0.2165	0.0687	0.1478	68.3	
Milwaukee	1975	0.1229	0.0404	0.0825	67.1	64.2
	1991	0.1907	0.0645	0.1262	66.2	
Minneapolis	1975	0.1167	0.0382	0.0784	67.2	46.8
	1991	0.1601	0.0613	0.0988	61.7	
St. Louis	1976	0.1356	0.0377	0.0978	72.2	62.8
	1989	0.2370	0.0754	0.1616	68.2	
South						
Atlanta	1975	0.1249	0.0258	0.0991	79.3	25.8
	1991	0.2003	0.0817	0.1185	59.2	
Baltimore	1975	0.1584	0.0371	0.1212	76.5	9.2
	1991	0.2024	0.0771	0.1253	61.9	
Houston	1974	0.1562	0.0550	0.1012	64.8	22.7
	1990	0.3113	0.1749	0.1364	43.8	
Miami	1975	0.1233	0.0304	0.0929	75.4	15.4
	1990	0.1821	0.0800	0.1020	56.0	

(continued)

Table 2.6   (continued)

Metropolitan area/years		Overall	Variance Between-group	Within-group	Within-group (% of overall)	ΔWithin-group/ ΔOverall (%)
West						
Anaheim	1975	0.1289	0.0249	0.1040	80.7	14.5
	1988	0.1885	0.0758	0.1127	59.8	
Los Angeles	1975	0.1238	0.0260	0.0978	79.0	57.1
	1988	0.1808	0.0529	0.1280	70.8	
San Diego	1974	0.1104	0.0312	0.0792	71.7	51.2
	1989	0.2001	0.0750	0.1251	62.5	
San Jose	1975	0.0899	0.0301	0.0598	66.5	60.0
	1988	0.1520	0.0549	0.0970	56.7	
Seattle	1974	0.0943	0.0398	0.0545	57.8	95.9
	1988	0.1719	0.0430	0.1289	75.0	

SOURCE: Author's calculations from the Area Wage Surveys. See the text for details.

tion in Table 2.6, the variance of the ln(real wage) is divided into the weighted average of the variance within the office-clerical, professional-technical, skilled maintenance, and material movement groups and into the weighted average of the relative wage between these groups. Table 2.6 also focuses on the data for the initial and final years for each area.

In general, the data in Table 2.6 are consistent with the results of earlier studies. The variance within occupational groups accounts for about two-thirds to three-quarters of the overall variance for most areas for the initial and final years. (The main exception is Houston, in 1990, where wage variance between occupations is slightly greater than the variance within occupations.) The indication is that the overall wage inequality for a given period primarily reflects the variance in wages within the groups, not variance in average wage levels between groups.

A look at the change in the overall variance in the log of the real wage from the mid 1970s to late 1980s, however, shows a different picture for a number of local labor markets in the sample. Clearly, changes both within and between groups occurred during that period. The final column in Table 2.6 shows the percentage of the change in the overall variance associated with the change in the variance within occupational groups. In Nassau–Suffolk, Cincinnati, Cleveland, Atlanta, Baltimore, Houston, Miami, and Anaheim, most of the rise in the overall variance came from changes in the relative wage between groups, not from changes in the variance within groups. Changes in the wage structure between the four groups appear to have been more important in the South and West. The wide range among urban areas suggests that a closer look at changes in the variance within groups and at changes in relative wage rates between groups is warranted.

WAGE INEQUALITY WITHIN OCCUPATIONAL GROUPS

Table 2.7 shows the variance of the log of the real hourly wage among workers within the four occupational groups in the AWS data for the initial and final year available for each metropolitan area. The variance is highest among workers in the less-skilled material movement group and lowest for those in skilled maintenance. Increased wage inequality appears across the board. Only six cells in Table 2.7 show a decrease in the variance over time: the estimated variance for office-clerical workers in Anaheim, Minneapolis, and San Diego and for professional-technical workers in Milwaukee decreased slightly between the initial and final years, and for material movement workers in Baltimore and Miami there was a slightly larger decrease.

There also appear to be considerable differences between occupational groups and among metropolitan labor markets in the levels of and the changes in the variance of real wage rates. This would suggest that in testing hypotheses about the causes of the changes in the wage variance, we can exploit those differences by examining the determinants of changes in the wage variance over time within a panel of occupational groups and metropolitan areas. Chapter 5 takes this approach.

RELATIVE WAGES OF OCCUPATIONAL GROUPS

As shown in the variance decompositions, changes in the average wage between the four occupational groups accounted for a substan-

Table 2.7   Variance in ln(Real Hourly Wage) by Occupational Group

Metropolitan area/years		Office-clerical	Professional-technical	Skilled maintenance	Material movement
Northeast					
Nassau–	1975	0.0473	0.0700	0.0224	0.1303
Suffolk	1987	0.0682	0.0929	0.0540	0.1804
New York	1975	0.0569	0.0812	0.0355	0.0833
	1989	0.1016	0.0970	0.0517	0.1432
Philadelphia	1976	0.0731	0.0795	0.0287	0.1144
	1988	0.0814	0.0948	0.0550	0.1927
Midwest					
Chicago	1974	0.0484	0.0692	0.0246	0.0969
	1986	0.0799	0.0775	0.0527	0.1648
Cincinnati	1974	0.0574	0.0668	0.0222	0.1397
	1989	0.0733	0.0896	0.0566	0.2092
Cleveland	1974	0.0595	0.0785	0.0254	0.1142
	1990	0.0887	0.0974	0.0494	0.2052
Detroit	1976	0.1024	0.0854	0.0082	0.0925
	1989	0.1148	0.0974	0.0206	0.2256
Indianapolis	1975	0.0861	0.0986	0.0331	0.1534
	1988	0.0887	0.1087	0.0665	0.2441
Milwaukee	1975	0.0584	0.0765	0.0234	0.1272
	1991	0.0669	0.0728	0.0486	0.2076
Minneapolis	1975	0.0576	0.0653	0.0200	0.1088
	1991	0.0570	0.0668	0.0403	0.1680
St. Louis	1976	0.0797	0.0811	0.0248	0.1455
	1989	0.1021	0.1001	0.0521	0.2724
South					
Atlanta	1975	0.0547	0.0783	0.0412	0.1482
	1991	0.0711	0.0869	0.0669	0.1657
Baltimore	1975	0.0721	0.0711	0.0347	0.1758
	1991	0.0834	0.0866	0.0511	0.1635
Houston	1974	0.0648	0.0702	0.0286	0.1516
	1990	0.0840	0.1013	0.0955	0.1806
Miami	1975	0.0565	0.0806	0.0776	0.1206
	1990	0.0726	0.1371	0.0977	0.1154

Table 2.7   (continued)

Metropolitan area/years		Office-clerical	Professional-technical	Skilled maintenance	Material movement
West					
Anaheim	1975	0.0636	0.0662	0.0230	0.1708
	1988	0.0575	0.0884	0.0675	0.1885
Los Angeles	1975	0.0622	0.0667	0.0290	0.1525
	1989	0.0689	0.0779	0.0635	0.1860
San Diego	1974	0.0657	0.0493	0.0168	0.1300
	1989	0.0628	0.0808	0.0270	0.1897
San Jose	1975	0.0477	0.0525	0.0119	0.0971
	1988	0.0600	0.0754	0.0875	0.1293
Seattle	1974	0.0527	0.0486	0.0110	0.0710
	1988	0.0667	0.0770	0.0799	0.2072

SOURCE: Author's calculations from the Area Wage Surveys.

tial portion of the increased wage variance over time in a number of urban areas. Table 2.8 takes a closer look at changes in the relative occupational wages for the sample of local labor markets. The table entries show the mean real hourly wage rate for workers in the office-clerical, professional-technical, and skilled maintenance groups as a percentage of the mean real hourly wage for workers in the material movement group in the initial and final years for each area.

The data in Table 2.8 suggest three major changes in the structure of relative occupational wages from the mid 1970s to the late 1980s. First, with the exception of professional-technical workers in Nassau–Suffolk and skilled maintenance workers in Miami, the relative wage of the three groups rose in every area during the period. Second, that rise was perhaps most striking in the case of office-clerical workers. In nine areas, clerical workers went from earning less, on average, than material movement workers to earning more, on average. Finally, in the mid 1970s, skilled maintenance workers had the highest relative wage in 16 of the metropolitan areas, but by the end of the 1980s, professional-technical workers had the highest relative average real wage in 16 of the 20 areas.

Table 2.8   Relative Wages,[a] by Occupational Group (%)

Metropolitan area/years		Office-clerical	Professional-technical	Skilled maintenance
Northeast				
Nassau–Suffolk	1975	97.9	148.4	147.7
	1987	98.9	140.4	144.8
New York	1975	105.7	165.7	142.5
	1989	125.4	197.6	150.6
Philadelphia	1976	80.1	124.0	128.5
	1988	106.8	172.8	159.3
Midwest				
Chicago	1974	87.3	133.3	142.7
	1986	95.8	155.3	159.3
Cincinnati	1974	91.7	130.0	148.7
	1989	114.8	189.5	166.9
Cleveland	1974	87.9	132.8	149.6
	1990	113.9	210.7	207.0
Detroit	1976	85.3	147.9	140.3
	1989	104.0	163.5	174.8
Indianapolis	1975	85.0	138.4	154.3
	1988	97.2	169.8	173.6
Milwaukee	1975	84.0	122.0	149.2
	1991	99.3	169.9	172.0
Minneapolis	1975	75.2	121.8	136.0
	1991	106.9	177.9	167.9
St. Louis	1976	84.5	128.6	145.0
	1989	112.1	186.6	185.3
South				
Atlanta	1975	106.9	152.5	165.2
	1991	127.4	213.7	166.8
Baltimore	1975	102.4	151.3	167.9
	1991	125.6	209.4	185.9
Houston	1974	122.7	173.7	191.1
	1990	172.4	296.5	243.2
Miami	1975	118.2	169.7	174.7
	1990	141.2	247.9	150.6
West				
Anaheim	1975	102.2	146.8	150.5
	1988	121.0	173.5	163.5

Table 2.8   (continued)

Metropolitan area/years		Office-clerical	Professional-technical	Skilled maintenance
West (continued)				
Los Angeles	1975	99.3	149.2	154.3
	1989	121.8	190.0	177.6
San Diego	1974	92.5	136.2	153.8
	1989	125.4	206.3	195.6
San Jose	1975	86.8	125.6	139.9
	1988	118.1	179.3	157.5
Seattle	1974	68.5	96.7	114.9
	1988	95.4	165.8	124.4

SOURCE: Author's calculations from the Area Wage Surveys.

[a] The numbers are the average real hourly wage in a given occupational group, as a percentage of the average real hourly wage of workers in the Material Movement group.

The data show a slightly different picture of changes in the relative wage of different groups than that seen in studies that measure skill differentials by changes in the average wage of college-educated workers relative to that of high school graduates or by changes in the relative wage of nonproduction versus production workers. Here, the evidence shows rising relative wages for clerical as well as for professional-technical workers. Since in the AWS data the latter are largely computer- and electronics-oriented workers, it is very possible that changes in the demand for computer skills and a growing demand for college-educated workers is behind the changes in their relative wages. But the simultaneous rise in the relative wage for clerical workers raises the question of the extent to which changing skill and educational requirements are driving these changes in wage inequality.

In addition, the relative wage of skilled maintenance workers rose considerably in most of the local labor markets, even if not as rapidly as the relative wage of professional-technical workers. And, the fact that the relative wage of skilled maintenance workers rose in many areas where their relative employment was falling casts some doubt on the widely accepted view that a steadily rising demand for skilled workers, driven largely by technological change, increased both the relative wage for and the relative employment of skilled workers. Given the findings in this chapter, that view has to be qualified in the case of skilled maintenance workers.

SUMMARY

This chapter has examined trends in the level and in the distribution of wages of workers in 41 jobs in four major occupational groups for 20 large metropolitan labor markets from 1974 to 1991. While there are considerable differences among the 20 areas and, often, between the four census divisions, the local labor market data taken from the Area Wage Surveys generally follows time patterns similar to those found in national data from the Current Population Survey. The median real hourly wage tended to be pro-cyclical, rising in the late 1970s, falling in the recessions of the early 1980s, rising again in the post-1984 recovery, and falling in the recession of 1990–1991. Wage inequality, measured by the variance in the logarithm of the real hourly wage and by the 75–50 and 50–25 log wage differences, rose steadily during the decade and a half under consideration.

The similarity in the findings from the AWS and the CPS is of considerable interest because the AWS data comes from surveys that over-sampled large employers and refer to the wages of full-time workers in a limited number of detailed job titles. Because the CPS data comes from surveys of individuals, and hourly wages are estimated from responses about annual earnings and hours worked, it is difficult to distinguish changes in wage practices from changes in the job patterns of individual workers. The AWS data suggests that there have indeed been substantial changes in the structure of real wages and that those changes are fairly widespread. The data examined in this chapter also reveal considerable differences among local labor markets in the timing and extent of changes in the wage structure. Metropolitan areas differ in the extent to which changes in wage inequality reflect changes in the relative wage of workers at the upper and lower quartiles of the distribution. The data also show considerable differences among metropolitan areas in the relative importance of wage variance within occupations as a source of increased wage inequality. The local labor markets in the sample show different patterns of change in the wage variance within occupations and in the relative wage between groups. These inter-urban differences are important in that the cross-section differences in wage structure changes between occupational groups and among urban areas, coupled with changes over time, provide a potentially rich data set, one that could prove more useful for evaluating some hypotheses than data bases that are restricted to information encompassing only differences in the wage structure over time.

Note

1. The CPI is the only inflation measure available for metropolitan areas. While considerable attention has been paid to measurement errors and biases in the CPI (Boskin et al. 1997), it is not clear that the available substitutes provide significantly more-reliable inflation indicators (Steindel 1997).

3 Trends in Benefit and Union Contract Coverage

This chapter considers trends in benefits and trends in union contract coverage. While nonwage benefits are an important part of worker compensation, few studies have examined the relationship between changes in benefit provisions and the rise in wage inequality. Houseman (1995) found that coverage by employer-provided health insurance and pension plans decreased the most between 1979 and 1993 for workers with the least education, which suggests that the trend in benefits worked to reinforce trends in the wage structure during the 1980s. Benedict and Shaw (1995) found that the dispersion of wages plus pension benefits was 2 percent higher than that of wages alone, because of the positive correlation between wage level, pension coverage, and pension value across workers. The national decline in union membership and contract coverage during the 1980s is widely documented and its impact on the wage distribution has been examined in a number of papers (for example, Freeman 1993). Here, I examine data on benefit coverage and union contract coverage from the Area Wage Surveys.

The AWS reported benefit and union contract coverage separately for full-time workers in the highly aggregated office worker and plant or production worker groups. While the office worker group closely matches the office-clerical group used to report wage data, the production worker group includes job titles beyond those in the skilled maintenance and material movement groups. For example, the production worker group includes fabricating, processing, assembling, and inspection, in addition to maintenance, shipping, receiving, warehousing, cleaning, and security work. The AWS excluded administrative, executive, professional, and part-time workers from both the office and the production worker groups. The differences in reporting mean that the trends analyzed here cannot be linked directly to the trends discussed in Chapter 2. However, general developments in benefit and union contract coverage are of interest in their own right and might provide insight into changes in the structure of nonwage compensation that complements our understanding of changes in the wage structure.

HOLIDAY AND VACATION TIME

Table 3.1 presents data on changes in time off from work for holidays and vacations for full-time office and plant workers. It shows the average number of days off for paid holidays, as reported by the employers surveyed in the AWS. The number of holidays shows little change, the most important perhaps being an increase in the number of holidays for office workers in the South and West, an increase that brought those workers on par with their counterparts in the Northeast and Midwest. The increase can be seen in the regional averages of the mean number of holidays. In the Northeast and Midwest, plant workers averaged 9.7 holidays in the mid 1970s and 9.6 holidays at the end of the 1980s; office workers in those two regions averaged 9.9 days and 9.8 days, respectively. Neither change is at all significant. In the South and West, plant workers averaged 8.4 holidays in both the mid 1970s and at the end of the 1980s, while the average number of holidays for office workers increased by half a day, from 9.0 to 9.5.

Table 3.1 also shows vacation time for workers with five years on the job, in particular the percentage of workers with vacations of two or fewer weeks per year. The data suggest a general improvement in the amount of vacation time, with the percentage falling in every case but that of production workers in San Diego. The change from the initial to final year in the percentage of workers having limited vacation averaged −24.4 percentage points for office workers and −11.6 points for production workers. Significant improvements in vacation time for plant workers were registered in Nassau–Suffolk, Cleveland, Minneapolis, and Seattle. For office workers, the biggest changes were in Nassau–Suffolk, Chicago, Minneapolis, Houston, and Seattle.

The results in Table 3.1 appear to be in line with those in Chapter 2, which show a rise in the relative pay of clerical workers vis-a-vis material movement workers. Table 3.1 also shows that benefits for office workers rose relative to those for skilled and unskilled plant workers.

Table 3.1 Holidays and Vacation Time for Full-Time Plant and Office Workers

Metropolitan area/years	Average number of holidays				Two or fewer weeks of vacation[a] (%)			
	Initial year		Final year		Initial year		Final year	
	Plant	Office	Plant	Office	Plant	Office	Plant	Office
Northeast								
Nassau–Suffolk 1975/1987	9.6	10.7	10.0	10.4	60	58	37	24
New York 1975/1989	10.1	10.9	10.3	10.2	40	30	37	25
Philadelphia 1976/1988	9.6	10.3	9.2	9.5	65	59	62	41
Midwest								
Chicago 1974/1986	9.4[b]	9.4[b]	9.6	9.6	67	71	56	41
Cincinnati 1974/1989	9.0[b]	9.3[b]	9.0	9.9	71	64	60	57
Cleveland 1974/1990	9.8	9.3	9.2	9.7	65	60	45	35
Detroit 1976/1989	11.3	11.0	10.6	10.8	32	48	25	32
Indianapolis 1975/1988	9.6	9.4	9.6	9.6	62	75	50	48
Milwaukee 1975/1991	10.0	9.9	10.0	9.4	65	62	62	36
Minneapolis 1975/1991	8.6	8.9	8.6	9.4	76	73	44	24
St. Louis 1976/1989	9.6	9.5	9.8	9.7	68	73	65	56
South								
Atlanta 1975/1991	7.8	8.9	8.3	9.3	69	64	55	47
Baltimore 1975/1991	8.6	9.3	8.3	9.3	74	69	64	43
Houston 1974/1990	7.7[b]	8.7[b]	7.6	9.0	75	71	53	29
Miami 1975/1990	6.9	7.9	7.2	8.9	69	64	62	45
West								
Anaheim 1975/1988	8.7	9.4	8.5	9.7	64	52	47	25
Los Angeles 1975/1989	8.8	9.2	8.9	9.9	55	51	43	31
San Diego 1974/1989	8.6	9.0	8.7	9.7	52	42	53	31
San Jose 1975/1988	9.3	9.5	9.6	10.1	40	41	37	24
Seattle 1974/1988	9.0[b]	9.5[b]	9.0	9.8	73	81	42	27

SOURCE: Area Wage Surveys.

[a] The vacation data is for workers with five years on the job with the current employer.

[b] 1977 data is the earliest available.

HEALTH INSURANCE

The extent to which workers are covered by employer-provided health insurance has been a significant part of the national debate on the reform of the health care industry. Table 3.2 presents data on the percentage of office and plant workers offered health insurance benefits and the percentage offered health insurance benefits that were fully paid for by the employer. The first point to note about this information is the very high rate of health insurance coverage provided by the employers surveyed by the AWS program in the 20 metropolitan areas. In contrast, Houseman's (1995) analysis of national data from the Current Population Survey showed that 36.8 percent of all workers in 1980 had no health insurance and that by 1989 this figure had risen to 42.7 percent. Only in the case of production workers in Miami in 1990 does the data reported in Table 3.2 come close to the rates of non-coverage found by Houseman, which undoubtedly reflects the fact that the firms included in the AWS are generally large ones that might be expected to offer a fuller array of benefits than smaller firms. Also, as we will see, the potential impact of unions on the workers in our sample is significantly higher than in the economy as a whole.

In our sample, the percentage of workers offered health insurance dropped slightly from the mid 1970s to the late 1980s. The average change in coverage was –6.5 percentage points for production workers and –2.4 points for office workers. While this might appear to be slim evidence for a substantial erosion of health insurance benefits, it should be noted that a few areas exhibited substantially larger changes than these overall averages. The percentage point change was –32 for Miami production workers, –22 for San Diego plant workers, –21 for Los Angeles plant workers, and –14 for Milwaukee office workers. Still, the evidence suggests a fairly high and stable rate of health insurance coverage for workers in most areas in the sample.

The right-hand columns of Table 3.2 show the percentage of workers with fully paid, employer-provided health insurance benefits. Again, the AWS data indicates a much larger percentage of workers with such benefits than is seen in national samples. Houseman (1995) reported CPS data showing that about 28 percent of workers in 1980 and 21 percent in 1989 had health insurance requiring no employee

Table 3.2 Health Insurance Coverage for Full-Time Plant and Office Workers[a] (%)

Metropolitan area/years	Workers covered				Noncontributory plans[a]			
	Initial year		Final year		Initial year		Final year	
	Plant	Office	Plant	Office	Plant	Office	Plant	Office
Northeast								
Nassau–Suffolk 1975/1987	89	96	98	99	82	71	70	58
New York 1975/1989	93	98	97	99	86	64	75	43
Philadelphia 1976/1988	97	99	94	99	86	70	65	54
Midwest								
Chicago 1974/1986	99	99	96	99	74	54	65	55
Cincinnati 1974/1989	94	97	94	97	74	69	60	48
Cleveland 1974/1990	95	96	93	97	85	66	63	37
Detroit 1976/1989	99	100	94	99	94	91	80	81
Indianapolis 1975/1988	96	98	93	99	72	65	61	58
Milwaukee 1975/1991	98	99	90	85	72	71	37	23
Minneapolis 1975/1991	96	98	84	89	82	64	35	32
St. Louis 1976/1989	97	99	96	99	80	57	67	43
South								
Atlanta 1975/1991	94	99	93	99	58	52	49	36
Baltimore 1975/1991	94	96	82	90	74	57	42	41
Houston 1974/1990	93	99	84	99	46	47	39	42
Miami 1975/1990	93	99	61	88	55	65	14	38
West								
Anaheim 1975/1988	96	99	85	98	78	56	47	52
Los Angeles 1975/1989	95	99	74	95	75	68	42	50
San Diego 1974/1989	97	99	75	91	76	67	40	43
San Jose 1975/1988	99	99	98	99	84	76	79	85
Seattle 1974/1988	98	99	99	99	91	63	81	72

SOURCE: Area Wage Surveys.
[a] Noncontributory plans are fully paid by the employer.

contributions to premiums. Table 3.2 shows a dramatic decrease in the percentage of workers with 100 percent employer-paid health insurance. The average change shown in Table 3.2 is –20.6 percentage points for production workers and –15.2 points for office workers; the only increases were for office workers in Chicago, San Jose, and Seattle. Again, the evidence for health insurance indicates that the relative position of office workers tended to improve.

PENSION COVERAGE

The percentage of workers offered pension plans and those with plans fully paid by the employer can be found in Table 3.3. Pension coverage in most areas in the sample is close to twice as high as the 45 percent reported by Houseman (1995), with the main exception being production workers in Miami. From the mid 1970s to the late 1980s, pension coverage generally fell for production workers and rose for office workers, although the changes were not pronounced. The

Table 3.3 Pension Coverage for Full-Time Plant and Office Workers (%)

Metropolitan area/years	Workers covered				Noncontributory plans[a]			
	Initial year		Final year		Initial Year		Final year	
	Plant	Office	Plant	Office	Plant	Office	Plant	Office
Northeast								
Nassau–Suffolk 1975/1987	76	85	76	86	73	77	69	78
New York 1975/1989	88	88	88	91	82	76	82	86
Philadelphia 1976/1988	88	89	68	91	83	82	58	75
Midwest								
Chicago 1974/1986	84	85	81	83	73	68	74	73
Cincinnati 1974/1989	81	91	80	93	73	85	73	81
Cleveland 1974/1990	88	88	80	90	83	80	75	81
Detroit 1976/1989	91	90	80	92	89	85	78	89
Indianapolis 1975/1988	84	90	78	95	74	81	73	89
Milwaukee 1975/1991	84	88	86	96	77	79	72	76
Minneapolis 1975/1991	87	85	87	92	82	75	67	78
St. Louis 1976/1989	89	83	93	96	84	73	85	83
South								
Atlanta 1975/1991	68	79	82	92	59	59	63	76
Baltimore 1975/1991	79	87	82	83	70	76	63	65
Houston 1974/1990	70	83	73	89	59	70	55	72
Miami 1975/1990	55	80	53	73	49	74	38	65
West								
Anaheim 1975/1988	70	80	68	88	59	64	53	69
Los Angeles 1975/1989	74	85	73	88	58	67	65	67
San Diego 1974/1989	78	73	71	88	70	61	53	64
San Jose 1975/1988	77	86	81	88	63	70	73	73
Seattle 1974/1988	90	91	87	90	82	82	77	77

SOURCE: Area Wage Surveys.
[a] Noncontributory plans are fully paid by employers.

average percentage point change across the 20 areas was –1.6 for plant workers and +3.9 for office workers. Pension coverage for production workers rose in 6 local labor markets, while that for office workers rose in 16.

A similar pattern can be seen in the percentage of workers with pensions requiring no employee contributions. That percentage fell for production workers, with the change averaging –5.8 percentage points, and rose slightly for office workers, with the change averaging +1.2 points. These data reinforce the conclusion that the structure of benefits changed in favor of office workers after the mid 1970s. They also strongly suggest that the change was evolutionary, not revolutionary, in its effect, with a high and relatively stable percentage of both office and production workers having employer-provided pensions. While there is evidence of inter-area differences in the levels and in changes in the provision of health insurance and pensions, the differences are not as pronounced as those seen in the wage distribution data in Chapter 2.

OTHER INSURANCE BENEFITS

The AWS noted workers covered by benefits other than vacations, health insurance, and pensions. Table 3.4 shows the changes over time in the percentage of plant and office workers covered by different insurance programs in each of the 20 metropolitan labor markets. While considerable differences are evident across the 20 markets, two general conclusions emerge. First, the data provide additional evidence of an improvement in benefits for office workers relative to those for production workers. Second, the percentage of workers offered long-term disability and dental insurance increased substantially in the decade and a half after 1975.

It appears, however, that the percentage of plant and office workers offered life insurance fell slightly during the sample period. This decrease, while indeed slight, was more pronounced for plant workers, particularly in Miami and Southern California. But coverage for accidental death and dismemberment rose in 9 areas for production workers and in 15 areas for office workers. Again, there were fairly

Table 3.4 Changes in Employer Coverage of Insurance Programs[a] (%)

Metropolitan area/years	Life		Accidental death & dismemberment		Sickness & accident		Long-term disability		Dental	
	Plant	Office	Plant	Office	Plant	Office	Plant	Office	Plant	Office
Northeast										
Nassau–Suffolk 1975/1987	+6	+3	+11	+6	+9	+12	+12	+27	+34	+48
New York 1975/1989	−3	+2	+2	+15	−16	+4	+11	+30	+46	+61
Philadelphia 1976/1988	−4	+2	+16	+13	−13	+9	−1	+10	+33	+47
Midwest										
Chicago 1974/1986	−1	0	+15	+18	−2	−1	+3	+11	+56	+66
Cincinnati 1974/1989	−3	+5	+9	+11	+4	+9	+9	+15	+52	+70
Cleveland 1974/1990	−9	−5	−10	+8	−8	+12	0	+21	+56	+78
Detroit 1976/1989	−8	0	−7	+4	−15	−11	0	+19	+22	+33
Indianapolis 1975/1988	−2	−1	0	+3	−20	+4	+5	+11	+35	+53
Milwaukee 1975/1991	0	−2	+7	+5	−1	+15	+13	+30	+54	+71
Minneapolis 1975/1991	−7	0	−1	+9	+14	+5	+16	+25	+53	+59
St. Louis 1976/1989	−2	0	+3	−7	−5		+10	+29	+27	+40
South										
Atlanta 1975/1991	−4	0	−3	−3	+11	+36	+15	+25	+51	+68
Baltimore 1975/1991	0	−3	+20	+4	0	+4	+10	+19	+43	+67
Houston 1974/1990	−4	−1	+15	+26	−3	+16	+19	+27	+60	+78
Miami 1975/1990	−22	−5	−15	+6	−13	+17	0	+27	+18	+69
West										
Anaheim 1975/1988	−18	0	−28	−18	+3	+3	−7	+8	+28	+38
Los Angeles 1975/1989	−11	0	−9	+4	−3	−19	−2	+6	+26	+45
San Diego 1974/1989	−16	−3	−16	−10	+7	+12	+7	+18	+31	+44
San Jose 1975/1988	−1	+1	−8	+4	−1	+8	−6	+6	+34	+39
Seattle 1974/1988	−2	+1	−1	−2	−2	+9	+9	−10	+23	+41
Average	−5.5	−0.3	0	+4.8	−2.7	+7.2	+6.1	+17.7	+39.1	+55.7

SOURCE: Area Wage Surveys.
[a] Numbers show the change in the percentage of workers covered by insurance between the initial and final year for each area.

large decreases in coverage for plant workers in Miami, Anaheim, and San Diego. In the case of sickness and accident insurance, the pattern is one of decreased availability for production workers and increased availability for office workers. For plant workers, the biggest drops in coverage were in New York, Indianapolis, Miami, and Philadelphia. While coverage for clerical workers rose in general, it dropped significantly in Indianapolis and Los Angeles. There appear to have been greater inter-urban differences in the coverage for life, accidental death and dismemberment, and sickness and accident insurance than we saw in the data for health insurance and pensions.

The percentage of workers covered by long-term disability insurance generally rose or remained constant from the mid 1970s to the late 1980s. On average, the increase in coverage for office workers was nearly three times greater than that for production workers. Finally, in all 20 areas, the percentage of office and production workers covered by dental insurance rose dramatically from the very low levels of the mid 1970s. Again, office workers clearly gained relative to production workers.

UNION CONTRACT COVERAGE

The field surveys conducted as part of the AWS program also inquire about the coverage of collective bargaining agreements. Published AWS reports data listed the percentage of office or plant workers in firms where a majority of office or plant workers were covered by union contracts. This measure of union influence is very different from data on union membership and goes beyond other union coverage data, since workers that met the criterion were included as covered, even if their individual terms and conditions of employment were not governed by a union contract. To the extent that the effects of a union contract spill over to nonunion workers in the same firm, this measure of union influence might perhaps best be regarded as a measure of the percentage of workers in the local labor market who are most likely to a have their wages and benefits influenced by collective bargaining.

Table 3.5 reports data on union contract coverage for the initial and final years for each of the 20 metropolitan labor markets. It also

Table 3.5 Union Contract Coverage for Full-Time Plant and Office Workers[a]

Metropolitan area/years	Initial year (%) Plant	Initial year (%) Office	Final year (%) Plant	Final year (%) Office	Percentage point change Plant	Percentage point change Office
Northeast						
Nassau–Suffolk 1975/1987	59	11	47	7	–12	–4
New York 1975/1989	81	14	79	21	–2	+7
Philadelphia 1976/1988	72	12	51	10	–11	–2
Midwest						
Chicago 1974/1986	72	13	58	15	–14	+2
Cincinnati 1974/1989	67	11	46	7	–21	–4
Cleveland 1974/1990	80	11	53	7	–27	–4
Detroit 1976/1989	89	17	62	17	–27	0
Indianapolis 1975/1988	66	8	46	5	–20	–3
Milwaukee 1975/1991	75	22	49	21	–26	–1
Minneapolis 1975/1991	71	11	38	6	–33	–4
St. Louis 1976/1989	82	15	76	10	–6	–5
South						
Atlanta 1975/1991	45	12	32	12	–13	0
Baltimore 1975/1991	63	18	40	12	–17	–6
Houston 1974/1990	40	6	24	5	–16	–1
Miami 1975/1990	30	8	13	9	–17	+1
West						
Anaheim 1975/1988	41	13	23	7	–18	–6
Los Angeles 1975/1989	56	16	40	9	–16	–7
San Diego 1974/1989	57	10	34	10	–23	0
San Jose 1975/1988	46	16	32	11	–14	–5
Seattle 1974/1988	91	22	65	28	–26	+6
Average	64.1	13.3	45.4	11.4	–18.0	–1.8

SOURCE: Area Wage Surveys.

[a]Figures show the percentage of full-time workers in firms where a majority of workers in each group were covered by union contracts.

shows the changes in union contract coverage over time and gives the average values for the 20-area sample. A substantially larger percentage of workers is counted as "covered" by (i.e., affected by) union contracts in this data than is seen in national data on union membership and union contract coverage. Here, contract coverage averaged close to two-thirds of production workers in the mid 1970s, with values over 80 percent for five metropolitan areas.

As is well known, union membership in the United States and in several other industrialized countries dropped sharply during the 1980s. As shown in Table 3.5, union contract coverage in the 20 labor markets also dropped sharply, even though union contract coverage for office workers in New York, Chicago, Miami, and Seattle rose slightly from the mid 1970s to the late 1980s. The drop in union contract coverage was most pronounced for plant workers in the industrialized Midwest, where it fell by 20 percentage points or more in Cincinnati, Cleveland, Detroit, Indianapolis, Milwaukee, and Minneapolis. San Diego and Seattle are the only areas outside the Midwest to have had declines of that magnitude. Union contract coverage appears to have dropped the least in the three areas in the Northeast, particularly in New York, where the rate of coverage for plant workers fell by 2 points and that for office workers rose by 7. Local trends in unionization thus appear to parallel national trends. However, considerable inter-urban variation in the level of and changes in contract coverage are evident in the data.

THE UNION INFLUENCE ON BENEFIT LEVELS

What is the relationship between inter-urban differences in union contract coverage and the percentage of workers offered various benefits? Given the evidence for a substantial drop in contract coverage over time, how has that relationship changed? Table 3.6 presents the results of a regression analysis of the effect of union contract coverage on the percentage of plant and office workers with health insurance, life insurance, a pension plan, and long-term disability insurance. Separate regressions were run on cross-section data for the initial and final years in the time series available for each city. There are 40 observations on the two worker groups across the 20 metropolitan areas. In addition to separate union contract coverage rate variables for office and plant workers, the regressions include as independent variables a dummy variable distinguishing plant from office employees and, to control for the net effect of area-specific measures, fixed effects for the 20 areas.

In general, the effect of union contract coverage on benefit coverage was substantially different for office and plant workers. For plant workers, the fraction covered by benefits increased with union cover-

Table 3.6   Regression Estimates for the Effect of Union Contract Coverage on Employee Coverage for Selected Benefits[a]

| Benefit | Constant | Union coverage | | Dummy for plant workers | R^2 |
		Plant workers	Office workers		
Health insurance					
First year	100.80*[b]	0.052*	−0.107	−7.46*	0.87
	(1.26)[c]	(0.018)	(0.066)	(0.862)	
Final year	90.69*	0.278*	−0.082	−20.53*	0.88
	(3.97)	(0.075)	(0.168)	(2.97)	
Pensions					
First year	79.87*	0.371*	0.322*	−24.64*	0.91
	(2.64)	(0.046)	(0.142)	(3.54)	
Final year	90.74*	0.281*	0.069	−23.53*	0.88
	(3.19)	(0.047)	(0.418)	(1.98)	
Life insurance					
First year	94.30*	0.092*	0.116	−6.81*	0.76
	(1.75)	(0.032)	(0.106)	(2.05)	
Final year	93.22*	0.277*	0.304*	−17.86*	0.86
	(2.26)	(0.065)	(0.092)	(2.91)	
Long-term disability insurance					
First year	52.76*	−0.025	−0.360	−27.53*	0.94
	(4.25)	(0.087)	(0.248)	(5.21)	
Final year	66.46*	0.1250	−0.155	−43.15*	0.93
	(6.73)	(0.1138)	(0.518)	(5.04)	

[a] The regressions labeled "first year" are estimated on 40 observations by type of worker and by metropolitan area for the first year available for each area. The regressions labeled "final year" are estimated for the final year available. All regressions include metropolitan-area fixed effects.

[b] * = significant at the 5% level.

[c] Heteroskedasticity-resistant standard errors are in parentheses.

age. For office workers, however, the variation among areas in union coverage did not correlate with the variation in the fraction of workers receiving benefits.

The regression estimates are similar for health and life insurance. Union contract coverage for plant workers has a statistically significant[1] positive relationship with the fraction of workers receiving these benefits. Interestingly, the estimated coefficients for union contract coverage are substantially larger in the final years. Apparently, the drop in union contract coverage was not accompanied by a drop in the union influence on these benefits. The magnitude of the coefficients suggests that a one-standard-deviation increase in union contract coverage would lead to a 7-point increase in the fraction of plant workers with health and life insurance in the late 1980s. The dummy variables for plant workers have a statistically significant negative effect on the fraction with health and life insurance, indicating that, other things being equal, office workers had higher rates of benefit coverage than did plant workers, and since the estimated coefficients are more than twice as large in absolute value in the final years, that advantage grew over time.

In the regression having pension plan coverage as the dependent variable, union contract coverage also has a statistically significant positive coefficient estimate. However, the estimated union effect is about the same in the initial and the final years and has a fairly large effect on the dependent variable. A one-standard-deviation increase in union contract coverage would add almost 13 points to plant worker pension coverage in the initial years and close to 8 points in the final years. Such increases would amount to a 15.5 percent increase over the mean value for pension coverage in the initial years and a 8.7 percent increase over the mean in the final years. Other factors held constant, the regressions also indicate that plant workers had substantially lower rates of pension coverage than did office workers. The coefficients for the plant dummy variables are very similar in the initial and final years, however, which suggests that the structure of pension coverage changed little over this period.

Finally, the regressions for long-term disability coverage indicate that union contract coverage had no statistically significant effect on the likelihood that workers would receive this benefit. For both the initial and the final years, the estimated coefficients are near zero and substantially less than their estimated standard errors. Again, the plant worker dummy variables indicate a strong advantage for office workers, one that increased from the mid 1970s to the late 1980s. In general, the results suggest that the extent of unionization had an important positive effect on the percentage of plant workers receiving several benefits.

Table 3.7 examines the effect of union contract coverage on the percentage of office and plant workers receiving fully paid health insurance and pension benefits. In the health insurance regression, the sharp drop in the constant term from the first to the second regression is consistent with the substantial erosion in health insurance benefits fully paid for by the employer seen in Table 3.2. Plant worker union con-

Table 3.7 The Effect of Union Contract Coverage on the Percentage of Workers Receiving Fully Paid Health Insurance and Pension Benefits[a]

Benefit	Constant	Union coverage Plant workers	Union coverage Office workers	Dummy for plant workers	R^2
Health Insurance					
First year	66.05*[b]	0.267*	−0.015	−6.30	0.89
	(4.93)[c]	(0.103)	(0.302)	(6.86)	
Final year	36.22*	0.553*	−0.073	−19.97*	0.91
	(7.53)	(0.111)	(0.428)	(3.90)	
Pensions					
First year	62.15*	0.431*	0.574	−22.94*	0.86
	(5.73)	(0.075)	(0.298)	(4.83)	
Final year	74.51*	0.301*	0.0001	−22.42*	0.91
	(3.96)	(0.063)	(0.1528)	(2.73)	

[a] The regressions labeled "first year" are estimated on 40 observations by type of worker and by metropolitan area for the first year available for each area. The regressions labeled "final year" are estimated for the final year available. All regressions include metropolitan-area fixed effects.

[b] * = significant at the 5% level.

[c] Heteroskedasticity-resistant standard errors are in parentheses.

tract coverage had a statistically significant effect on the incidence of employer-paid health plans, with the estimated effect rising over time. In the regression for the final years, a 10 percent increase in union contract coverage would be associated with a 2.5 percent increase in the fraction of plant workers in health plans that did not require worker co-payments. As in the regressions reported in Table 3.6, office worker union contract coverage was not significantly correlated with the fraction of workers with fully paid health plans.

Plant worker union contract coverage is also statistically significant and positively correlated with the fraction of workers with pension plans in which the employer pays 100 percent of the premiums. Office worker union contract coverage is statistically significant and positively correlated with fully paid pension plans in the regression for the initial years, but it is not in the regression for the final years. In general, the regression analyses reported in Tables 3.6 and 3.7 show that plant workers lagged behind office workers in benefit coverage, but that disadvantage was offset to some extent by the higher rates of unionization and the greater union-benefit effects for plant workers.

SUMMARY

An analysis of the AWS data on benefits reveals important changes in benefit coverage from the mid 1970s to the early 1990s. However, the nature of those changes varied considerably by metropolitan area and by type of benefit. Perhaps the conclusion to be drawn is that the evidence points to a relative shift in benefit coverage away from plant workers and toward office workers. In many cases, this relative shift also represented an absolute decrease in the fraction of plant workers receiving various benefits. The absolute decrease was perhaps most pronounced in Miami, where the fraction of plant workers receiving benefits generally fell substantially.

While we cannot directly tie the benefit coverage data in the AWS to the wage data described in Chapter 2, the tendency toward greater benefit advantage for office workers is at least consistent with one important feature of the rise in wage inequality. Recall from Chapter 2 the sharp rise in the average wage of office-clerical and professional-technical workers relative to that of material movement workers. Recall also that a few studies reviewed in Chapter 1 found evidence of sharp increases in the relative wage of nonproduction workers in manufacturing during the 1980s. The analysis in this chapter suggests that increases in the relative wages for office workers were accompanied by an increase in the relative availability of various benefits for these workers.

The AWS data also yield information on the extent of union influence on local labor markets. Because the specific measure employed includes workers who might not have been union members or who might not have been covered by explicit union contracts, the estimates for plant worker union contract coverage reported here are substantially higher than those drawn from the CPS or from union membership rolls. The union data from the AWS do follow the national trend toward lower union contract coverage rates over time. Estimates of the effects that inter-area differences in unionization have on various benefits indicates that greater union coverage was associated with higher fractions of plant workers with life insurance, health insurance, and pension plans. Unionization had no significant effect, however, on the benefits received by office workers.

Note

1.   Unless otherwise stated, statistical significance is at the 5 percent level.

4 Skill Requirements and Returns on Skills

Underlying the dramatic increase in wage inequality over the past two decades is a marked change in the price paid for skills and in the skills required by employers. The evidence points to sharp increases during the 1980s in the wage returns on schooling and on potential labor market experience (Buchinsky 1994), on cognitive skills in addition to schooling (Murnane, Willett, and Levy 1995), and on specific technical skills, such as the ability to use computers on the job (Krueger 1993). The evidence that wage inequality has increased for workers with a given level of education and that the returns on schooling are higher and growing more rapidly for workers at the upper reaches of the wage distribution (Buchinsky 1994) has also been taken as a sign of increased wage returns on unmeasured skills (Juhn, Murphy, and Pierce 1993).

The evidence also indicates that the demand for labor has shifted substantially in the direction of skilled workers, as seen in data showing that the level of education has risen over time (Wolff 1995), that required job-specific skills have increased (Cappelli 1993), and that the distribution of employment by occupation and by industry has shifted toward jobs requiring higher skills (Gittleman and Howell 1995). There is considerable interest in determining the relative importance of international trade and technological change in the rising demand for skilled workers. And, there is some question about the impact skill upgrading had on the 1980s rise in wage inequality, given the empirical evidence that skill upgrading rose more rapidly in the 1970s than in the 1980s (Howell 1994; Mishel and Bernstein 1996) and given the theory favoring the conclusion that rising average skill levels are associated with reduced wage inequality (Teulings 1995).

This chapter examines the evidence for changes in the returns on skills and in the relative demand for skills in the sample of 20 local labor markets. Since the AWS data measured job-specific wage rates and provided no information on the characteristics of the workers in those jobs, we cannot examine increases in the returns on skills through a traditional human capital model. Instead, we turn to an older model

61

of wage determination, one in which wages are attached to jobs and are determined largely by the relative skill requirements of those jobs. With this model, we can examine how average wage levels across occupations and among local labor markets responded to the skill characteristics of those occupations at different times. We can also use occupational skill measures to determine whether the skill mix within the four job groups covered by the AWS changed during the 1980s.

OCCUPATIONAL SKILL INDICES

The most comprehensive data on skill requirements is the *Dictionary of Occupational Titles* (U.S. Department of Labor 1991). Field examiners for the Department of Labor rated each job title by the level of skill required for the job. The ratings reflect many dimensions of skill, including the amount of education and training required, the physical and environmental demands of the job, the levels of cognitive, interactive, and language skills involved, and the degree of responsibility for machine operations. While the *Dictionary* has its limitations (see Miller et al. 1980), it does allow for a more comprehensive study of the returns on various job-specific skills than does a human capital model, restricted as it is to data on schooling and potential work experience as measures of skill.

Table 4.1 presents skill data selected from the *Dictionary* for each job title in the four occupational groups covered by the Area Wage Surveys. Skills are represented by three separate measures: specific vocational preparation, general educational development, and the worker functions required for each job.

Specific vocational preparation refers to the time the average worker needs to learn the techniques, acquire the information, and develop the ability to be an average performer. This preparation includes vocational education; apprenticeship, in-plant, and on-the-job training; and experience acquired in other jobs. Specific vocational preparation is measured according to the following nine-point scale (Gamboa, Gibson, and Holland 1994):

1. Short demonstration
2. Less than one month

3. Over 1 month and up to 3 months

4. Over 3 months and up to 6 months

5. Over 6 months and up to 1 year

6. Over 1 year and up to 2 years

7. Over 2 years and up to 4 years

8. Over 4 years and up to 10 years

9. Over 10 years

In the AWS data, on this scale, the job titles range from a low of 2 for shipping packers to a high of 8 for maintenance electricians and tool-and-die makers. It is interesting that the required training time is high for the skilled maintenance workers and for the professional-technical workers in our sample. Most job titles in the two groups require two to four years or more of training. In contrast, most office-clerical jobs require less than six months of vocational preparation, and six of the nine material movement jobs in the sample require but one to three months. The result for this variable highlights one of the advantages of using occupation-based skill data as a supplement to worker educational attainment in measuring skill. It is unlikely that the long vocational preparation required for workers in skilled maintenance jobs would be adequately measured by years of schooling alone.

General educational development (GED) attempts to characterize the cognitive skills that are usually associated with formal education. Jobs are rated on a scale of 1 to 6 for levels of reasoning, mathematics, and language development. Reasoning development ranges from 1 (for jobs requiring only that the worker carry out instructions) to 6 (for jobs requiring logical or scientific thinking). Mathematics development runs from 1 (for jobs requiring basic arithmetic) to 6 (for jobs requiring advanced calculus, algebra, and/or statistics). Language development ranges from 1 to 6, depending on the degree of reading comprehension and oral communication skills needed for the job.

In our sample, the lowest-rated job titles (with ratings of 2 for reasoning and 1 for both mathematics and language) are shipping-packer, fork-lift operator, material-handling laborer, and general maintenance worker. Table 4.1 shows a clear ranking, with professional-technical

Table 4.1 Skill Measures for Job Titles by Occupational Group[a]

Occupational group/job	Specific vocational preparation	General educational development			Worker functions		
		Reasoning	Mathematics	Language	Data	People	Things
Office-Clerical							
Accounting clerk	5	4	3	3	4	8	2
File clerk	3	3	1	2	3	8	7
Key entry operator	4	3	2	3	5	8	2
Messenger	2	2	1	2	6	7	7
Order clerk	4	3	3	3	3	6	2
Payroll clerk	4	4	3	3	3	8	2
Receptionist	4	3	2	3	3	6	7
Secretary	6	4	3	4	3	6	2
Stenographer	5	3	2	3	3	6	2
Switchboard operator	3	3	2	3	6	6	2
Typist	3	3	2	3	5	8	2
Word processor	5	3	2	3	3	8	2
Professional-Technical							
Computer operator	6	4	2	3	3	6	2
Computer programmer	7	5	4	5	0	6	2
Computer systems analyst	7	5	4	5	1	6	7
Drafter	7	5	5	4	2	6	1
Electronics technician	7	5	5	4	1	6	1
Registered industrial nurse	7	5	4	5	3	7	4
Skilled Maintenance							
Carpenter	7	4	4	3	2	8	1
Electrician	8	4	4	4	2	6	1

Table 4.1 (continued)

General maintenance	3	2	1	1	3	8	4
Machine-tool operator	7	4	4	4	2	8	0
Maintenance mechanic	6	4	3	3	2	8	0
Motor vehicle mechanic	7	4	3	3	2	8	1
Millwright	7	4	3	3	2	8	1
Painter	7	3	2	2	3	8	1
Pipefitter	7	4	4	3	2	6	1
Stationary engineer	7	4	4	3	3	8	1
Tool & die maker	8	4	4	4	2	6	0
Trades helper	4	2	1	2	6	8	4
Material Movement							
Guard	3	3	1	2	6	6	7
Janitor	3	3	2	3	6	6	4
Material handling laborer	3	2	1	1	6	8	3
Order filler	3	3	2	2	4	8	7
Fork-lift operator	3	2	1	1	6	8	3
Shipper/receiver	5	3	3	2	3	8	7
Warehouseman	4	3	3	2	3	8	7
Truck driver							
Light/medium	3	3	2	2	6	8	3
Heavy/tractor trailer	4	3	2	2	6	6	3
Shipping packer	2	2	1	1	5	8	7

SOURCE: U.S. Department of Labor 1991.
[a] See the text for an explanation of the skill measures and codes

jobs requiring the highest GED levels and material movement jobs requiring the lowest. The distinction between the professional-technical and the skilled maintenance groups is much sharper than it was for vocational training. However, skilled maintenance jobs still require fairly high degrees of reasoning and mathematics skills.

Worker function ratings assess the requirements for dealing with data, people, and things. In contrast to the other skill indices in the table, worker functions involving more complex responsibility and judgment are assigned lower rather than higher numbers. Various jobs are rated according to the scales in Table 4.2 (U.S. Department of Labor 1991).

Professional-technical jobs require the highest skill level for data-related tasks, with the typical job requiring data coordination and analysis. While the worker function ratings related to data are generally lower for skilled maintenance than for professional-technical jobs, eight of the job titles within the skilled maintenance group do require data analysis.

No group in our sample requires high skill levels for the "people" variable. The jobs in the sample mainly require speaking/signaling and serving, tasks at the bottom of the scale of people-related functions, which undoubtedly reflects the fact that none of the groups covered by the AWS included strictly managerial jobs, which carry the highest people ratings.

Skilled maintenance jobs have the highest worker function ratings for tasks related to things (machines). The values for this measure indicate that precision work and operating-controlling skills are char-

Table 4.2   Worker Function Scale

Rating	Data	People	Things
0	Synthesizing	Mentoring	Setting up
1	Coordinating	Negotiating	Precision working
2	Analyzing	Instructing	Operating-controlling
3	Compiling	Supervising	Driving-operating
4	Computing	Diverting	Manipulating
5	Copying	Persuading	Tending
6	Comparing	Signaling	Feeding-offbearing
7		Serving	Handling
8		Taking instructions	

acteristic of the typical skilled maintenance job. Drafters and electronic technicians (from the professional-technical group) also have
high machine-related worker function ratings.

As might be expected, there is a close correlation among most of
the skill measures reported in Table 4.1. The three GED measures are
highly interrelated, with correlation coefficients ranging from 0.81 to
0.89 for the 40 job titles in the four occupational groups. Specific
vocational preparation is also highly correlated with GED reasoning
($r = 0.81$), GED mathematics ($r = 0.83$) and worker functions related
to data ($r = -0.78$) measures. Because of these close correlations and
the uniformly low levels for the worker functions–people measure, the
analysis of the returns on skill in the next section narrows its focus to
specific vocational preparation, language development, and relationship to things.

RETURNS ON SKILL

If the skill measures described above accurately portray the skill
requirements for various jobs, the difference in ratings across jobs
should be reflected in average wage levels. Data are available in the
AWS on the average wages paid to male and female workers in specific job categories in manufacturing and nonmanufacturing in each of
the 20 areas in our sample. The AWS data can be used to determine
the extent to which average wages reflect the skill requirements linked
to specific job categories by the *Dictionary* data and to study the evidence for changes over time in the relationship between job-specific
wages and skill requirements. This analysis focuses on the estimated
parameters of

Eq. 4.1 $\ln W_{ij} = \beta_1 S_i + \beta_2 X_j + e_{ij}$

The dependent variable in this equation is the logarithm of average real hourly wages for male or female workers in manufacturing or
nonmanufacturing establishments in job title i and local labor market
j. Vector S_i includes various *Dictionary* skill measures for the ith occupation. Vector X_j controls for the effect of other determinants of the

average wage in job i and area j. Finally, e represents a random error term.

Of the 20 metropolitan areas in the sample, 16 have AWS data for both the late 1970s and the late 1980s. Since these were periods of economic expansion a decade apart, the analysis of changes in the returns on skill during the 1980s is limited to these 16 areas. For both the late 1970s and the late 1980s, there are over 1,000 observations on average hourly wages for job titles, by sex and by industry cells, across the 16 local labor markets in the sample. The areas and years included in this analysis are

Anaheim	1978, 1988	Milwaukee	1978, 1987
Atlanta	1978, 1987	Minneapolis	1978, 1987
Baltimore	1978, 1987	Nassau–Suffolk	1978, 1987
Cincinnati	1979, 1989	New York	1978, 1989
Detroit	1979, 1989	Philadelphia	1979, 1988
Indianapolis	1978, 1988	St. Louis	1979, 1989
Los Angeles	1978, 1989	San Jose	1978, 1988
Miami	1978, 1987	Seattle	1979, 1988

Independent Variables

Four independent variables are included in the vector X_j to control for wage determinants in addition to skill requirements. The first is a dummy variable indicating whether workers in a particular job were employed in manufacturing. The second is a dummy variable that differentiates male from female workers. The third independent variable is the measure of union contract coverage found in the AWS (discussed in Chapter 3). The AWS reported estimates of the proportion of workers in firms where a majority of workers were covered by union contracts. The AWS also reported data on aggregate plant and aggregate office worker groups separately for each local labor market, by manufacturing and nonmanufacturing industry. Each job title falling in, for example, the office worker category in manufacturing in a given area would have the same value for the union contract coverage variable. The fourth independent variable in X_j is the local rate of occupational unemployment for the year preceding the relevant AWS survey. This variable is also an aggregate measure matching the four AWS occupational categories. Appendix C gives details on the source and characteristics of the unemployment rate variable.

The vector of job-specific skill requirements in the wage model includes six different variables. The first, taken from the *Dictionary* but not yet discussed, is a measure of the physical demands of the job. This dummy variable differentiates jobs that require moderate or heavy work, as measured by the exertion of force needed to perform the tasks involved (see Gamboa, Gibson, and Holland 1994) from jobs characterized by light or sedentary work.

The second skill variable in the model comes from the AWS. A number of the office-clerical and professional-technical jobs and a few material movement jobs have wage data reported for various job levels. For example, average hourly wage data were reported for Secretaries I, II, III, IV, and V. The job levels distinguish between workers who perform the same basic job but whose tasks involve differing degrees of experience, responsibility, and supervisory duties. Four dummy variables are included, to indicate whether a specific observation was for a job at the first, second, third, or higher level for a specific job title. The reference group for the job-level dummy variables is all workers in jobs with just one job level reported in the AWS.

Dummy variables are also used to examine the effect that different levels of required vocational preparation have on the average wage for a given job and in a given local labor market. Separate variables indicate jobs requiring 6 to 12 months of specific vocational preparation, jobs requiring 1 to 2 years of preparation, and jobs requiring 2 or more years. The reference job for these dummy variables requires six months or less of specific vocational training.

The level of GED language development required for each job is another skill requirement used in the model. Recall that GED requirements usually reflect skills acquired through formal education and that the three GED measures in the *Dictionary* data are all highly correlated across the job titles in the sample. Thus, while the variables used in the regressions refer explicitly to language skills, they can also be interpreted as indicators of the education required. The model includes three dummy GED variables: GED1 indicates jobs that require the ability to read rules and procedures, to write reports, and to speak before an audience; GED2 indicates those that require the ability to read journals and manuals, to write business letters and reports, and to participate in panel discussions; and GED3 indicates jobs that require the ability to read technical and financial reports and legal documents, to write speeches, manuals, and critiques, and to use effective and persuasive speech. Jobs requiring basic reading, writing, and speaking skills form the reference group.[1]

Two dummy variables are used to measure job requirements in relationship to working with machines (worker functions–things). One designates jobs that require operating, controlling, or driving machinery; the second designates jobs that require machine set-up and precision work. Jobs associated with handling, tending, or feeding machinery are in the reference group.

The final job-related skill measure is available only for the regressions estimated for 1987 to 1989. Alan Krueger has kindly supplied CPS data on the proportion of workers using computers in each three-digit census occupation in 1984 and 1989 from his study of the effect of computer use on wages (Krueger 1993). The average of the 1984 and 1989 data serves as an independent variable in alternate regressions for the late 1980s.

Regression Results

The results from ordinary least squares (OLS) regressions estimated separately for 1978–1979 and 1987–1989 are reported in Table 4.3. The skill requirements and other wage determinants, including metropolitan-area fixed effects, explain about 70 percent of the variation in average wages across jobs, by sex, by industry, and by urban area cells in the two periods. Almost all the estimated coefficients are statistically significant, with signs that are logically consistent. Finally, a comparison of the results for the two periods supports the conclusion that the wage returns on skills changed significantly during the 1980s.

The coefficients for the manufacturing dummy variable indicate that workers in that sector enjoyed a wage advantage of about 3 percent when compared with those in nonmanufacturing jobs in the late 1970s. In the late 1980s sample, however, the estimated wage effect from working in manufacturing is not significantly different from zero. The result supports the argument that increased foreign and domestic competition in the manufacturing sector during the 1980s lowered rents and the share of rents captured by workers (Sachs and Shatz 1996).

Table 4.3 Skill Requirements and Other Determinants of Wages, by Job and by Area, All Workers[a]

	1978–79		1987–89		
Variable	Coefficient	Mean	Coefficient[b]	Coefficient	Mean
Constant	1.7200*[c]	—	1.7412*	1.6980*	—
	(0.0233)[d]		(0.0397)	(0.0400)	
Manufacturing	0.0301*	0.5238	−0.0020	−0.0027	0.5255
	(0.0083)		(0.0147)	(0.0115)	
Male	0.1531*	0.5603	0.1087*	0.1072*	0.5075
	(0.0126)		(0.0175)	(0.0175)	
Union	0.0032*	33.51	0.0037*	0.0039*	27.16
	(0.0004)		(0.0005)	(0.0005)	
% Unemployed	−0.0058*	6.94	−0.0152*	−0.0134*	4.86
	(0.0024)		(0.0046)	(0.0045)	
Physical	0.0546*	0.359	0.1304*	0.1418*	0.3434
demands	(0.0247)		(0.0462)	(0.0325)	
Job level 1	−0.1707*	0.1785	−0.1293*	−0.1507*	0.1623
	(0.0166)		(0.0238)	(0.0273)	
Job level 2	−0.0141	0.1961	0.0037	−0.0177	0.1858
	(0.0159)		(0.0225)	(0.0254)	
Job level 3	0.0580*	0.0912	0.1043*	0.0851*	0.1
	(0.0218)		(0.0280)	(0.0296)	
Job level 4	0.1642*	0.0684	0.2517*	0.2388*	0.0632
	(0.0231)		(0.0281)	(0.0296)	
Voc. prep.,	0.0962*	0.1251	−0.0038	−0.0014	0.1566
6 mo. to 1 yr.	(0.0112)		(0.0155)	(0.0016)	
Voc. prep.,	0.1058*	0.1609	0.0960*	0.0877*	0.1472
1 to 2 yr.	(0.0129)		(0.0175)	(0.0175)	
Voc. prep.,	0.0334	0.2417	0.0998*	0.1064*	0.2208
2 to 4 yr.	(0.0174)		(0.0254)	(0.0246)	
GED 1	0.0624*	0.4397	0.0849*	0.0771*	0.4792
	(0.0166)		(0.0228)	(0.0232)	
GED 2	0.0721*	0.1876	0.1745*	0.1736*	0.1774
	(0.0208)		(0.0297)	(0.0292)	
GED 3	0.5518*	0.0873	0.5890*	0.5513*	0.0858
	(0.0275)		(0.0396)	(0.0438)	

(continued)

Table 4.3   (continued)

| | 1978–79 | | 1987–89 | | |
Variable	Coefficient	Mean	Coefficient[b]	Coefficient	Mean
Machine	0.1511*	0.5283	0.1002*	0.0965*	0.5396
operation	(0.0145)		(0.0198)	(0.0199)	
Machine set-up	0.2014*	0.1837	0.1169*	0.1220*	0.1575
	(0.0252)		(0.0362)	(0.0350)	
Computer use	—	—	—	0.0010*	46.39
				(0.0004)	
R^2	0.73		0.7	0.7	

[a] The mean of the dependent variable is 2.1708 for 1978–79 and 2.1380 for 1987–89. There are 1,535 observations for 1978–79 and 1,060 for 1987–89. All regressions include metropolitan-area fixed effects.
[b] Excluding computer use variables.
[c] * = significant at the 5% level.
[d] Heteroskedasticity-resistant standard errors are in parentheses.

The wage advantage accruing to men is also lower in the 1980s regression than in that estimated for the 1978–1979 cross-section data. Other things being equal, men earned about 16.5 percent more than women in the late 1970s and 11.5 percent more than women in the late 1980s.[2] Evidence of improvement in the relative standing of women during the 1980s had been found in a number of earlier studies.

The estimated wage effect of union contract coverage rose slightly from 1978–1979 to 1987–1989, even though the percentage of workers in firms where a majority of workers were under contract fell from 33.5 percent to 27.2 percent. This result appears to be inconsistent with the evidence on union wage concessions during the 1980s (Voos 1994) and with evidence from the United Kingdom on falling union wage differentials accompanying the decline in union membership (Stewart 1995). However, Linneman, Wachter, and Carter (1990) found that the union wage advantage in the United States may have risen slightly during the 1980s from already high levels in the late 1970s.

The unemployment rate results are consistent with other studies on the wage curve (Blanchflower and Oswald 1994) and with evidence that wages became more responsive to labor market forces during the

1980s (Eberts and Groshen 1991). The indications are that a one-point rise in the local rate of occupational unemployment would have lowered the average occupational wage by 0.6 percent in the late 1970s and by close to 1.5 percent in the late 1980s, other things being equal.

When the results for the late 1980s are compared with those for the late 1970s, the coefficient estimates for the skill variables generally change in a way that can be interpreted as evidence for an increase in the returns on skill. For example, the estimated coefficient for the dummy variable "physical demands" (identifying jobs requiring moderate to heavy physical exertion) is more than twice as great in the 1980s regression. Workers in jobs requiring moderate to heavy exertion had a wage advantage of 5.6 percent in the late 1970s and almost 14 percent in the late 1980s.

The estimates for the job-level coefficients bear close scrutiny. The negative coefficients for Level-1 jobs suggest that workers in these jobs earned significantly less than the average wage for jobs with only one level in the AWS. Those in Level-2 jobs earned about the same, on average, as workers in jobs without job-level designations. Finally, workers in Level-3 and Level-4 (or higher jobs) earned higher wages, on average, than workers in jobs without levels. The pattern of coefficients for these four variables indicates that the marginal wage effect of the job level rose with the level and that the marginal wage effect for Levels 3 and 4 rose substantially between the late 1970s and late 1980s.

The pattern of change in the estimated wage returns on vocational preparation is more complex. These returns fell for workers in jobs requiring the least training. During the 1980s, jobs requiring six months to one year of training became indistinguishable, in wage terms, from jobs requiring less than six months of training. Further, the estimated coefficient for jobs requiring one to two years of specific vocational preparation also is slightly smaller in the regression for the late 1980s. Only the results for the dummy variable for jobs requiring over two years of specific vocational preparation are consistent with the rising-returns-on-skill argument. The wage advantage, on average, for workers in job requiring more than two years of training increased from 3.4 percent in the late 1970s to 10.9 percent in the late 1980s.

The estimated parameters for the three language development variables (GED1, GED2, and GED3) indicate that higher skill levels were associated with greater marginal wage effects in both the late 1970s and the late 1980s and that the wage returns on language skills rose for all three levels from the 1970s to 1980s. Recall that the language development variable is highly correlated with math and reasoning development across the occupations in our sample and that all three variables measure skills generally acquired through formal education. Thus, the changes noted in Table 4.3 in the wage effect of GED1, GED2, and GED3 offer further evidence of increasing wage returns on language, math, and reasoning skills (Murnane, Willett, and Levy 1995). The estimated returns on skill for jobs requiring the highest GED level is 74 percent for the regression for the late 1970s and about 80 percent for the regression for the late 1980s.

While there is evidence of an increased wage advantage during the 1980s for workers in jobs requiring the most training, higher language development, and greater levels of responsibility, the wage advantage for those with machine-related skills is estimated to have declined between the late 1970s and the late 1980s, as can be seen in the smaller estimated coefficients for the machine operator and the machine set-up variables in the regression for the late 1980s. The coefficients indicate that the average wage in jobs requiring machine-operation skills was 16.3 percent higher than that for machine-tending in the late 1970s and 10.5 percent higher in the late 1980s, other things being held constant. The wage advantage for machine set-up skills relative to machine-tending skills was 22.3 percent in the late 1970s and 12.4 percent in the late 1980s. Clearly, the argument that technological change and other labor-market forces increased the returns on skills during the 1980s needs to be qualified.

The addition of the variable measuring the extent of computer use in a given job changes the estimated coefficients for the other independent variables in the 1987–1989 regression only slightly. The computer-use variable itself has a statistically significant positive correlation with the average hourly wage for a given job by gender, by industry, and by area cell, lending support to Krueger's (1993) conclusion that computer skills were particularly relevant in the 1980s, a relevance reflected in a wage advantage for workers with that skill.

The regression results reported in Table 4.3 indicate that firms in the 20 local labor markets generally paid more for various measures of worker skill at the end of the 1980s than they did at the beginning of that decade. The only exceptions are found in the estimated wage response for jobs requiring six months to one year and one to two years of specific vocational preparation and in the wage advantage associated with machine-operation and set-up skills. The largest increases in the wage returns on skill during the 1980s were in the jobs requiring the longest training and the highest GED levels.

Regression Results, by Sex

Given the differences between the labor market experience of men and women during the 1980s (Blau and Kahn 1994), it is useful to examine estimates of the model by sex. Chow tests yield F statistics that reject the null hypothesis of common regression coefficients for men and women and support the estimation of separate regressions for each. The results for men are reported in Table 4.4 and those for women in Table 4.5.

The results for men generally support the main conclusions of the analysis for all workers, although there are some interesting differences. The estimated effect of the manufacturing industry on wage rates for men is not statistically different from zero in the late 1970s or in the late 1980s. The estimated response of male wages to local rates of occupational unemployment is substantially smaller in the regressions for the late 1980s, particularly when computer use is added to the equation. The job-level dummy variables are generally not statistically significant determinants of male wage rates, perhaps because the job-level designations in the AWS are most prevalent among office-clerical jobs.

The regressions for men do indicate a substantial increase in the wage advantage associated with higher job requirements for specific vocational preparation and for the GED language level. And, like the results for all workers, the regressions for men also indicate that the wage advantage for skills associated with machine operation and set-up were lower in the regression for the late 1980s than in that for the late 1970s. Finally, the proportion of workers using computers on the job has a statistically significant positive effect on the average wage for men, by industry and by area cells in the 1987–1989 sample.

The regression results for women (Table 4.5) also support the conclusion of rising returns on skill during the 1980s. They also reveal some interesting differences in comparison with the estimates for all workers and for male workers.

Table 4.4   Skill Requirements and Other Determinants of Wages, by Job and by Area, Men[a]

Variable	1978–1979		1987–1989		
	Coefficient	Mean	Coefficient[b]	Coefficient	Mean
Constant	1.9670*[c]	—	1.9483*	1.9069*	—
	(0.0462)[d]		(0.0632)	(0.0641)	
Manufacturing	–0.0135	0.5733	–0.0250	–0.0236	0.5911
	(0.0140)		(0.0199)	(0.0199)	
Union	0.0035*	46.32	0.0032*	0.0033*	38.83
	(0.0005)		(0.0007)	(0.0007)	
% Unemployed	–0.0092*	7.88	–0.0071	–0.0056	5.47
	(0.0030)		(0.0057)	(0.0045)	
Physical	0.0345	0.5919	0.0422	0.0485	0.6115
demands	(0.0388)		(0.0422)	(0.0414)	
Job level 1	–0.2117*	0.0826	–0.1954*	–0.2183*	0.0781
	(0.0496)		(0.0679)	(0.0726)	
Job level 2	0.0024	0.1221	–0.1304*	–0.1526*	0.1059
	(0.0446)		(0.0599)	(0.0632)	
Job level 3	0.0763	0.1035	–0.0417	0.0612	0.5085
	(0.0493)		(0.0632)	(0.0659)	
Job level 4	0.1680*	0.0558	0.0599	0.0489	0.3450
	(0.0525)		(0.0634)	(0.0628)	
Voc. prep.,	0.0719*	0.0988	–0.0544	–0.0784*	0.1022
6 mo. to 1 yr.	(0.0231)		(0.0295)	(0.0309)	
Voc. prep.,	0.0038	0.0953	0.0837	0.0213	0.0554
1 to 2 yr.	(0.0299)		(0.0437)	(0.0512)	
Voc. prep.,	–0.0207	0.3802	0.0825*	0.0662	0.3550
2 to 4 yr.	(0.0253)		(0.0347)	(0.0347)	
GED 1	0.0804*	0.3198	0.1092*	0.1059*	0.3253
	(0.0249)		(0.0323)	(0.0324)	
GED 2	0.0218	0.1698	0.1786*	0.1412*	0.1561
	(0.0339)		(0.0490)	(0.0529)	
GED 3	0.5247*	0.1116	0.6513*	0.5945*	0.1004
	(0.0370)		(0.0492)	(0.0594)	
Machine	0.1400*	0.3570	0.0862*	0.0909*	0.3401
operation	(0.0213)		(0.0213)	(0.0302)	

Table 4.4   (continued)

Variable	1978–1979		1987–1989		
	Coefficient	Mean	Coefficient[b]	Coefficient	Mean
Machine	0.2310*	0.3209	0.1603*	0.1965*	0.3048
set-up	(0.0317)		(0.0433)	(0.0476)	
Computer use	—	—	—	0.0013*	32.98
				(0.0007)	
R^2	0.59		0.59	0.60	

[a] The mean of the dependent variable is 2.3056 for 1978–79 and 2.2599 for 1987–89. There are 860 observations for 1978–79 and 538 for 1987–89. All regressions include metropolitan-area fixed effects.
[b] Excluding computer use variables.
[c] * = significant at the 5% level.
[d] Heteroskedasticity-resistant standard errors are in parentheses.

In contrast to the results for men, women employed in manufacturing earned significantly higher wages than those working in nonmanufacturing in both the late 1970s and the late 1980s. The estimated wage advantage for the manufacturing industry did fall from around 8 percent in the 1978–1979 sample to 3.5 percent in the later period.

The regressions for women also indicate that the wage effect associated with union contract coverage was smaller in the late 1980s. In addition, the local rate of occupational unemployment did not have a statistically significant impact on women's wage rates in either period.

The estimated coefficients for skill variables follow a pattern for women somewhat similar to that for all workers. The wage advantages associated with the physical exertion required in a job, with the highest job levels (in those jobs with level data reported by the AWS), and with the most training required all increased during the 1980s. In contrast, the wage effect of the highest GED level in the late 1980s was substantially lower than that estimated for the late 1970s.

Because only a small number of women work in jobs requiring machine set-up and operation, the two machine-related dummy variables were combined for the regressions for women. The results indi-

Table 4.5   Skill Requirements and Other Determinants of Wages, by Job and by Area, Women[a]

| Variable | 1978–1979 | | 1987–1989 | | |
	Coefficient	Mean	Coefficient[b]	Coefficient	Mean
Constant	1.6046*[c]	—	1.7232*	1.5421*	—
	(0.0308)[d]		(0.0617)	(0.0659)	
Manufacturing	0.0782*	0.4607	0.0341*	0.0346*	0.4579
	(0.0095)		(0.0126)	(0.0116)	
Union	0.0039*	17.19	0.0022*	0.0017	15.14
	(0.0007)		(0.0010)	(0.0009)	
% Unemployed	0.0008	5.73	–0.0181	–0.0089	4.22
	(0.0057)		(0.0100)	(0.0099)	
Physical	–0.0911	0.0622	0.1736*	0.2766*	0.0670
demands	(0.0510)		(0.0893)	(0.0804)	
Job level 1	–0.1311*	0.3007	–0.1116*	–0.2174*	0.2490
	(0.0157)		(0.0218)	(0.0240)	
Job level 2	0.0269	0.2919	0.0412	–0.0650*	0.2680
	(0.0157)		(0.0226)	(0.0260)	
Job level 3	0.0880*	0.0756	0.1688*	0.0624*	0.1111
	(0.0225)		(0.0282)	(0.0291)	
Job level 4	0.1952*	0.0844	0.3304*	0.2280*	0.0900
	(0.0220)		(0.0280)	(0.0299)	
Voc. prep.,	0.1022*	0.1585	0.0173	0.1263*	0.2126
6 mo. to 1 yr.	(0.0122)		(0.0174)	(0.0271)	
Voc. prep.,	0.1465*	0.2444	0.1285*	0.0577	0.2184
1 to 2 yr.	(0.0264)		(0.0324)	(0.0331)	
Voc. prep.,	0.1252	0.0652	0.3021*	0.1516*	0.0824
2 to 4 yr.	(0.0645)		(0.1225)	(0.0771)	
GED 1	0.0825*	0.5926	0.0782*	0.0262	0.6379
	(0.0208)		(0.0347)	(0.0355)	
GED 2	0.0627*	0.2104	0.1121*	0.2251*	0.1992
	(0.0338)		(0.0451)	(0.0483)	
GED 3	0.5383*	0.0563	0.3862*	0.3843*	0.0709
	(0.0684)		(0.1266)	(0.0818)	

Table 4.5 (continued)

| Variable | 1978–1979 | | 1987–1989 | | |
	Coefficient	Mean	Coefficient[b]	Coefficient	Mean
Machine operation and set-up	0.1332* (0.0194)	0.7556	0.0907* (0.0249)	–0.0034 (0.0294)	0.7510
Computer use	—	—	—	0.0049* (0.0007)	60.21
R^2	0.81		0.76	0.79	

[a] The mean of the dependent variable is 1.999 for 1978–79 and 2.0124 for 1987–89. There are 675 observations for 1978–79 and 522 for 1987–89. All regressions include metropolitan-area fixed effects.
[b] Excluding computer use variables.
[c] * = significant at the 5% level.
[d] Heteroskedasticity-resistant standard errors are in parentheses.

cate that the wage advantage associated with these skills dropped from the late 1970s to the late 1980s.

The estimated coefficients of the wage regression for female workers are greatly affected by including the computer-use variable in the model. Statistically speaking, perhaps the biggest effect is to drive the estimated coefficient of the machine-related dummy variable to zero. Apparently, in the late 1980s, computer use on the job was the most relevant machine-related skill for determining women's wages. Computer use itself had a much more important positive effect on women's wages than it had on men's.

Including the computer-use variable also reduces the estimated coefficients for the dummy variables for jobs requiring one to two years and two or more years of specific vocational preparation and reduces those for the job-level dummy variables. One might speculate that the introduction of computer technology has eroded the value that employers place on some skills gained through lengthy training or through experience in lower-level jobs. Such skill substitution might be more pronounced in predominantly female office-clerical jobs where computer use has probably changed work the most.

The results for both men and women suggest that changes in the price paid for skills during the 1980s were perhaps more complex than is suggested by traditional human capital models, which focus on the returns on schooling and on potential experience. Returns on some levels of skill, like those associated with machine operation, fell during the 1980s. And, at least for women, computer use on the job may have lowered the returns on other skills and raised the wages for those who could use computers.

TRENDS IN THE SKILL MIX, BY OCCUPATIONAL GROUP

Along with a tendency toward higher wage returns on skill, researchers have also noted a rise in the average skill level of the U.S. workforce during the 1980s. Rising average skill levels have come about because of changes in industry and in patterns of employment, leading to an increase in the relative importance of skilled workers (Gittleman 1994), and because of increases in the skills required for a given job (Cappelli 1993). This pattern of rising returns on skill, accompanied by the rising relative employment of the skilled, is a key factor in analyzing the impact of technological change on the wage structure (Berman, Bound, and Griliches 1994).

Table 4.6 summarizes data on changes in the skill mix, by aggregate occupational group, for each of the 20 local labor markets in this study. The table reports the percentage change in the weighted average months of specific vocational preparation (SVP) between the initial and final years for the jobs in each group and in each area. For each job, we use the midpoint of the time range identified for each SVP code; for example, jobs with a code of 5 are assigned nine months of required preparation. Since the measure of skill is constant, changes in the skill index reflect changes in employment patterns across jobs requiring different skills within each occupational group. A positive percentage change indicates that employment within a group has shifted over time to higher-skill jobs.

Despite considerable differences across the 20 local labor markets, two trends are clear in Table 4.6. Three groups show a rise in the skill mix. Averaged across all 20 areas, the weighted average of the vocational preparation measure rose 10.2 percent for office-clerical workers, 2.5 percent for material movement workers, and 1.9 percent for

Table 4.6   Change in the Weighted Average of the Specific Vocational Preparation Index, by Occupational Group (%)

Metropolitan area/years	Office- Clerical	Professional- Technical	Skilled Maintenance	Material Movement
Northeast				
Nassau–Suffolk 1975/1987	−8.9	1.4	−40.9	7.4
New York 1975/1989	7.8	5.7	−32.9	−4.0
Philadelphia 1976/1988	1.4	4.2	−11.1	−2.9
Midwest				
Chicago 1974/1986	7.4	3.3	−2.7	1.5
Cincinnati 1974/1989	47.1	3.5	−14.6	16.5
Cleveland 1974/1990	12.3	3.2	−7.1	2.1
Detroit 1976/1989	23.8	3.7	0.2	1.4
Indianapolis 1975/1988	−6.6	3.3	−12.7	2.1
Milwaukee 1975/1991	4.2	7.4	−10.5	3.1
Minneapolis 1975/1991	15.1	3.2	−23.0	10.7
St. Louis 1976/1989	26.7	6.0	−1.2	8.7
South				
Atlanta 1975/1991	1.3	−2.7	−24.0	8.6
Baltimore 1975/1991	10.9	−1.8	−0.1	0
Houston 1974/1990	16.1	5.6	−14.1	−2.9
Miami 1975/1990	9.7	4.6	−54.7	−7.1
West				
Anaheim 1975/1988	3.9	0.2	−12.3	−6.2
Los Angeles 1975/1989	10.4	1.4	−17.5	1.8
San Diego 1974/1989	6.8	−0.5	−19.1	−8.2
San Jose 1975/1988	17.1	−0.3	−18.5	4.3
Seattle 1974/1988	5.7	−0.7	−27.3	2.0
Mean	10.2	1.9	−17.2	2.5

SOURCE: Area Wage Surveys and the *Dictionary of Occupational Titles'* training data.

professional-technical workers. Perhaps what is most striking is the sharp 17.2 percent <u>decline</u> in the average required months of vocational preparation within the skilled maintenance group.

Table 4.7 provides more complete information on the trends in the weighted average of months of specific vocational preparation for the 20 labor markets as a whole. The entries in Table 4.7 are the estimated slope coefficients for each occupational group from the following regression equation:

Eq. 4.2 $\ln \text{SVP}_{it}^{J} = \alpha_i + \beta \text{YEAR} + e_{it}$

in which the dependent variable, the logarithm of the weighted average months of vocational preparation required for jobs in occupation J and area i during period t, is a function of an area fixed effect and a trend term.

Controlling for inter-area differences shows evidence of a statistically significant positive trend in the SVP measure for the office-clerical and professional-technical groups. The data suggest that shifts in the job mix within these groups resulted in a 0.7 percent annual rate of increase in the SVP for office-clerical workers and a 0.15 percent annual rate of increase for professional-technical workers.

The positive shift, however, is restricted to the two white-collar groups. The trend coefficient is <u>negative</u> and statistically significant for skilled maintenance workers and not significantly different from zero for material movement workers. The SVP fell by −1.7 percent each year for skilled maintenance workers from 1974 to 1991.

The combined effects of increases in the mix of skills required for office-clerical and for professional-technical jobs and rising returns on skill help explain the increased relative wage reported for these two groups in Table 2.6. These combined effects are consistent with a relative improvement in benefits for office-clerical workers (discussed in Chapter 3). In general, the skill, wage, and benefit findings for the office-clerical and professional-technical groups support earlier studies that found a positive relationship between the relative earnings and employment of nonproduction workers and various measures of technological change.[3]

The results for skilled maintenance workers are somewhat surprising, although Howell (1995) found that the share of employment

Table 4.7 Trend Effects on the Average Number of Months of Specific Vocational Preparation Required for Each Occupational Group[a]

	Office-clerical	Professional-technical	Skilled maintenance	Material movement
β	0.0069*[b]	0.0015*	−0.0177*	0.0003
	(0.0011)[c]	(0.0004)	(0.0021)	(0.0011)
$\bar{R}^2$	0.64	0.56	0.60	0.55

[a] All regressions include metropolitan-area fixed effects.
[b] * = significant at the 5% level.
[c] Heteroskedasticity-resistant standard errors are in parentheses.

in high-skill, blue-collar jobs fell relative to the share of low-skill, blue-collar jobs in both manufacturing and nonmanufacturing industries from 1985 to 1990. A reduction in the average skill level required for skilled maintenance jobs and in the wage return on machine-control skills are the types of changes one might expect from machine-tool computerization and other aspects of the widespread redesign of the American workplace since the mid 1980s (Applebaum and Batt 1994). The changes in the skill mix and in the returns on machine-related skills are partly responsible for the slower growth in the relative wage for skilled maintenance workers relative to office-clerical and professional-technical groups (see Table 2.6). The next chapter looks more closely at the determinants of changes in relative wage levels in our sample of local occupational labor markets.

SUMMARY

The major shift in the position of skilled workers in the U.S. economy is an important element in the changes in the wage structure over the past two decades. The wage advantage of skilled workers has increased substantially, and the demand for labor appears to have shifted markedly toward skilled and away from unskilled workers. To date, most of the discussion of these shifts has focused on relative returns and on employment opportunities for more-educated workers. The occupational focus of the Area Wage Survey data permits a broader look at the role that skills play in the 20 local labor markets under study. Using the skill information in the *Dictionary of Occupational Titles*, we are able to examine occupational skills in terms of the training, cognitive skills, and responsibility for machine operations required.

This chapter offers two insights. First, the evidence shows that the wage returns on several dimensions of skill rose sharply from the late 1970s to the late 1980s, particularly for jobs requiring higher levels of training, cognitive skills, and responsibility. In contrast, the wage differential for jobs requiring greater responsibility for setting up and operating machinery, a traditional blue-collar and clerical skill, appears to have fallen significantly during that decade. This is particularly evident in the wage regressions for women when we control for computer use on the job.

Second, employment shifts from the mid 1970s to the early 1990s generally worked to increase the relative importance of jobs requiring more training. The main exception is the case of skilled maintenance workers, for whom employment appears to have shifted in favor of jobs requiring less training. The evidence for wage returns on skill and for the relative mix of job skills indicates that skilled blue-collar jobs in the 20 local labor markets may not have followed the general U.S. trend toward greater returns on skill and toward more employment opportunities for the most skilled worker

Notes

1. The GED rating for each job is on a scale from 1 to 6. The reference group for jobs requiring basic reading skills combines those jobs with a GED language rating of 1 or 2. My GED1 variable includes jobs with a 3 rating; my GED2 variable indicates jobs with a 4 rating, and my GED3 variable indicates jobs with a 5 rating. None of the job titles in the sample carried a rating of 6 on the GED language scale.

2. In semilogarithmic regressions like these, the coefficients of dummy variables must be adjusted in order to correctly calculate the proportionate change in the dependent variable. If b is the coefficient on a dummy variable X, then the percent change in the dependent variable associated with $X = 1$ versus $X = 0$ is $(e^b - 1) \times 100$, where e is the base of natural logarithms. So the proportionate

wage advantage for men in the late 1970s using the regressions in Table 4.2 is $(e^{0.1531} - 1) \times 100 = 16.5\%$. For more details on this adjustment, see Thornton and Innes (1989).

3. See, for example, Berman, Bound and Griliches (1994), Howell and Wolff (1992), and Bernard and Jensen (1997).

5 Market and Institutional Factors in Rising Wage Inequality

One important open question about the causes of rising U.S. wage inequality is the relative importance of market versus institutional factors. The sharp decline in trade union membership and the falling real value of the minimum wage during the 1980s has led some observers to emphasize these institutional factors as determinants of the simultaneous rise in wage inequality. Institutional factors also seem to be of primary importance in explaining international differences in wage inequality, since market factors, especially those related to technological change and international trade, are likely to have common effects in all industrialized countries (see Freeman 1996). This chapter examines the relative importance of labor market factors, as well as changes in unionization and the minimum wage, in explaining the growth of wage inequality in the sample of 20 local labor markets.

The results in Chapter 2 show that changes over time in the variance of the logarithm of the real wage for all workers in the sample can be traced to changes in both the relative wage across and the variance within the four occupational clusters included in the AWS data. Given the importance of these two sources of change, this chapter focuses on an analysis of the determinants of the changes in the average occupational wage and the variance of wage rates within occupations over time. In addition, because much of the interest in changes in the wage distribution is motivated by concern over the relative wages earned by the lowest-paid workers, this chapter also examines the factors associated with changes in the wage differential between workers at the median and at the 25th percentile of the occupational wage distribution.

Previous studies have had difficulty in assessing the relative importance of market and institutional factors because of database limitations. Time-series databases for a single country covering a short time span may not be adequate to fully capture slowly changing institutional factors, and databases limited to cross-sectional information cannot capture market dynamics. Our panel data set, with its considerable variation among occupations and metropolitan areas and its variation over time within these occupations and areas, can potentially overcome these limitations of earlier databases.

METHOD

The analysis in this chapter treats the panel database as a sample of 80 local occupational labor markets (4 occupational groups times 20 cities) observed at various points from 1974 to 1991. First, the analysis assumes that, at least in the short run, there are significant barriers to mobility between local occupational labor markets as well as barriers to mobility among metropolitan areas. This seems to be a reasonable assumption, given the four groups reported on in the AWS. In the short run, it is easy to think of truck drivers, secretaries, computer programmers, and maintenance electricians as sellers of labor in distinct labor markets. Because the model of the changes in the wage structure in these 80 local occupational labor markets is a dynamic one, the initial time series observation for each market is lost to lags, leaving 364 observations in the panel database.

A second assumption in this analysis is that the parameters of the wage structure model are constant across the 80 local occupational markets. This assumption permits the full use of the cross-sectional variation in the data set to estimate the parameters. While it might be interesting to investigate parameter differences between occupations or between metropolitan areas, that investigation is beyond the scope of this study.

The analysis of the role of market and institutional factors in shaping changes in the wage structure in local occupational labor markets is based upon the general single-equation dynamic model (Eq. 5.1). Hendry, Pagan, and Sargan (1984) showed that such a model, generalized to include any lag length, encompasses the commonly employed single-equation dynamic models found in the literature:

Eq. 5.1 $Y_{it} = \alpha Y_{it-1} + \beta_1 X_{it} + \beta_2 X_{it-1} + e_{it} + d_i + f_t$

where the subscript i designates a particular occupation in a given metropolitan area. The model includes group effects (d_i) and period effects (f_t) that could be important in analyzing the panel data. An important question is whether to model the group and period effects as fixed or random effects. Hsiao (1986) showed that in a dynamic model with the lagged dependent variable on the right-hand side of the equation, the least-squares dummy variable approach to estimating fixed group and period effects may seriously bias the estimate of α in a downward direction. Since the generalized least squares (GLS) estimator used in the random effects model is not subject to such a bias, it is the preferred panel estimator for this type of model.

For greater ease of interpretation and to reduce the possibility of multi-collinearity in its estimation, the model is rewritten as

Eq. 5.2 $\quad Y_{it} = \alpha Y_{it-k} + \beta_1 (X_{it} - X_{it-k}) + (\beta_1 + \beta_2) X_{it-k} + e_{it}$
$$+\ d_i + f_t$$

Here the effects on Y_{it} of the independent variables included in X_i are divided into a level effect, measuring the impact on Y_{it} of a constantly maintained level of X_i over time, and a change effect, measuring the impact on Y_{it} of a change in the level of X_i over time. This is useful because it is not clear *a priori* whether it is the level of an institutional variable or its change that matters for the distribution of wages (Gottschalk 1996).

Equation 5.2 also recognizes that the length of the lag between observations in the panel is longer than one year for most variables. The length of time between AWS site visits was usually three years but varied from two to four years in the sample. The variable lag is shown by $t - k$ in Equation 5.2. To control for the effects of variation in this interval, all estimates of the model include the number of years in the interval between t and $t - k$ as a right-hand-side variable (see Hausman, Lo, and MacKinlay 1992).

The analysis looks at three dependent variables. The first set of regressions uses the logarithm of the average real wage in the local occupational labor market as the dependent variable. These regressions attempt to estimate the effect of the variables included in the vector X on the changes in the relative wage level across occupations from 1975 to 1991. A second set of regressions uses the variance of the logarithm of the real wage in the local occupational labor market as the dependent variable. These regressions are used to analyze the determinants of changes over time in the distribution of wages within occupations and within metropolitan areas. The final set of regressions uses the difference between the logarithm of the real wage at the 50th and the 25th percentiles of the wage distribution in the local market as the dependent variable. These results can shed some light on the causes of changes in the relative position of low-wage earners within specific occupations.

A point of considerable interest is whether the estimates of the parameter α indicate the presence of an error-correction mechanism in the model. If α is positive but significantly less than 1, there is evidence of error-correction in the sense that a shock to Y_t would be dissipated to some extent over the following k years. The fundamental supply-and-demand model of the labor market predicts such an effect, based on the hypothesis that a short-run rise in the real wage would attract workers and, by increasing labor supply, would lower the wage over time. Similar effects might be seen with a rise in wage inequality. For example, the 1997 *Economic Report of the President* looks at how college enrollments have increased in response to the sharp rise in the college wage advantage during the 1980s, with the effect of lowering that advantage in recent years. If there were an error-correction mechanism in the model, that would be consistent with the generally accepted view that medium-term adjustments work to offset, at least in part, the wage effects of short-run labor market shocks.

The model uses the unemployment rate for experienced workers in each occupation and metropolitan area to capture short-run market factors. This is the same unemployment rate used in the regressions in Chapter 4, and Appendix C describes the sources and characteristics of this data. Since the unemployment rate captures the net short-run effect of supply-and-demand changes in the local occupational labor market, the level effect is measured for the period $t-1$ rather than for $t-k$. Bartik (1994, 1996) and Karoly and Klerman (1994) showed that more rapid growth and falling unemployment in local and regional labor markets are associated with reduced wage and income inequality. An article by Uchitelle (1997) suggested that falling unemployment in the United States during 1996 and 1997 resulted in rising real wages for the lowest-paid workers and reduced wage inequality. While we expect the local unemployment rate to reflect structural changes in labor demand (Hyclak 1996), to reflect the impact of foreign trade on domestic markets (Haveman 1997), and to capture the net effect of other short-run supply-and-demand changes in the labor market, this variable cannot be used to separate the effects of or to assess the relative importance of trade versus technology on the wage structure.

Included in vector X_i of the independent variables is the measure of union contract coverage (discussed in detail in Chapter 3). The AWS data reports the proportion of white-collar and blue-collar workers in firms where at least half of the workers were covered by union contracts. The union contract coverage variable for office workers serves as a measure of union coverage for both the office-clerical and the professional-technical workers in a given metropolitan area. Similarly, the local estimate of union contract coverage for plant workers serves as a measure of union coverage for both the skilled maintenance and the material movement workers in a given area. Again, the AWS measure of union contract coverage is a significantly broader measure of potential union wage influence than union membership or contract coverage rates would be.

In the regressions explaining the changes in the variance of wages and the changes in the 50–25 wage differential within local occupational labor markets, the impact of the minimum wage is measured by the minimum wage for the corresponding state relative to the average hourly wage in the local occupational labor market. The minimum wage data are taken from Neumark and Wascher (1992) and Nelson (1990, 1991, 1992). This relative measure of the importance of the minimum wage in a local occupational labor market cannot be used in the regressions having the logarithm of the average real wage as the dependent variable, because doing so would be equivalent to placing the inverse of the dependent variable on the right-hand side of the equation. In these regressions, then, the effect of the minimum wage is measured by the logarithm of the real minimum wage, in which the state-specific minimum wage is deflated by the CPI-W price index for the relevant metropolitan area. To allow for the differential effects of the minimum wage, the logarithm of the real minimum wage is interacted with dummy variables for each occupation.

The independent variables include measures designed primarily to control for two composition effects: changes over time in the relative importance of specific job titles within an occupational group for a given metropolitan area and changes in the industry mix of firms included in the AWS. The model controls for these composition effects in a way that might yield additional insights into the causes of change in the dependent variables.

The control variable for changes in the mix of workers by job title measures the weighted average skill level of the job titles within each local occupation. The skill level for each job title is measured by the midpoint of the range of months of the specific vocational preparation required for the job (see Chapter 4). Since this variable changes over time only if the relative proportion of workers in each job title changes, it can control for composition effects within occupations. The variable also provides a measure of the effect of shifts toward more-skilled or less-skilled jobs within occupations on the level and the distribution of wages in the local occupational labor market.

The control variable for the industry mix is also measured by a weighted average summing, across the six industrial categories included in the AWS, the products of the industry share of total employment and the 1984 industry-specific compensation effect estimated by Krueger and Summers (1988). This variable has the same value for all four occupational groups in a given area for a given year and changes over time only if the industry mix of the firms surveyed by the AWS changed. Thus, the variable accounts for changes in the industry mix in each area and period and also controls for one estimate of the effect of industry on compensation practices.

AN ANALYSIS OF THE REAL WAGE LEVEL

The first application of the model is analyzing the factors affecting the level of the logarithm of the average real hourly wage in the panel of local occupational labor markets. The interest here is in determining the role of market and institutional factors in explaining the widening of the gap between relative wages among occupations noted in Chapter 2. That widening gap played an important role in the overall trend toward greater urban wage inequality during the 1980s.

Table 5.1 reports three estimates of the real wage model plus some descriptive statistics. The three estimates are an ordinary least squares (OLS) regression without group or period effects; a generalized least squares (GLS), random-effects model, with a group effect only for each of the 80 local occupational markets in the cross-sectional portion of the

Table 5.1 Determinants of the Average Real Wage[a]

Variable	OLS	GLS (group)	GLS (group & time)	Mean, std. dev.
Constant	0.1055	0.1297	–0.0919	
	(0.0878)	(0.0750)	(0.1084)	
ln(Real Wage)$_{t-k}$	0.8095*[b]	0.7630*	0.8020*	2.2019
	(0.0388)	(0.0348)	(0.0368)	0.2500
	[0.7700]	[0.7258]	[0.7629]	
Δ% Unemployed$_t$	–0.0031*	–0.0032*	–0.0013	–0.2679
	(0.0013)	(0.0010)	(0.0011)	2.8442
	[–0.0335]	[–0.0346]	[–0.0141]	
% Unemployed$_{t-1}$	–0.0010	–0.0012	–0.0038*	6.8923
	(0.0012)	(0.0010)	(0.0011)	4.8850
	[–0.0223]	[–0.0223]	[–0.0706]	
Δln(Skill)$_t$	0.2572*	0.2682*	0.3136*	–0.0048
	(0.0418)	(0.0346)	(0.0367)	0.0824
	[0.0806]	[0.0221]	[0.0983]	
ln(Skill)$_{t-k}$	0.1419*	0.1687*	0.1581*	2.6208
	(0.0325)	(0.0284)	(0.0276)	1.0556
	[0.5699]	[0.6776]	[0.6350]	
ΔIndustry mix$_t$	–0.0078*	–0.0078	0.0105*	–0.3462
	(0.0029)	(0.0049)	(0.0027)	1.2068
	[–0.0358]	[–0.0358]	[0.0482]	
Industry mix$_{t-k}$	0.0009	0.0016	0.0043	6.0973
	(0.0023)	(0.0021)	(0.0022)	1.6639
	[0.0056]	[0.0101]	[0.0272]	
ΔUnion$_t$	0.0019*	0.0018*	0.0021*	–2.1819
	(0.0007)	(0.0006)	(0.0005)	4.8302
	[0.0349]	[0.0331]	[0.0386]	
Union$_{t-k}$	0.0009*	0.0011*	0.0007*	33.6500
	(0.0003)	(0.0003)	(0.0003)	26.3625
	[0.0903]	[0.1103]	[0.0702]	
Δln RMW$_t$ × OFFICE$_t$	–0.0302	–0.0132	0.1857*	–0.0166
	(0.0849)	(0.0696)	(0.0853)	0.0469
	[–0.0054]	[–0.0006]	[0.0331]	
ln RMW$_{t-k}$ × OFFICE$_{t-k}$	–0.0561	–0.0523*	–0.0092	0.3233
	(0.0347)	(0.0290)	(0.0759)	0.5637
	[–0.1203]	[–0.1122]	[–0.0197]	

(continued)

Table 5.1　(continued)

Variable	OLS	GLS (group)	GLS (group & time)	Mean, std. dev.
$\Delta \ln RMW_t$	−0.0287	−0.0150	0.1742*	−0.0166
× $TECH_t$	(0.0847)	(0.0694)	(0.0854)	0.0469
	[−0.0051]	[−0.0027]	[0.0311]	
$\ln RMW_{t-k}$	−0.1160*	−0.1240*	−0.0887	0.3233
× $TECH_{t-k}$	(0.0401)	(0.0334)	(0.0772)	0.5637
	[−0.2488]	[−0.2660]	[−0.1902]	
$\Delta \ln RMW_t$	0.1101	0.1041	0.2740*	−0.0166
× $SKILL_t$	(0.0853)	(0.0699)	(0.0847)	0.0469
	[0.0196]	[0.0186]	[0.0489]	
$\ln RMW_{t-k}$	−0.1615*	−0.1764*	−0.1185	0.3233
× $SKILL_{t-k}$	(0.0428)	(0.0360)	(0.0771)	0.5637
	[−0.3464]	[−0.3784]	[−0.2542]	
$\Delta \ln RMW_t$	0.1960*	0.2068*	0.4063*	−0.0166
× $MATER_t$	(0.0851)	(0.0697)	(0.0840)	0.0469
	[0.0349]	[0.0369]	[0.0725]	
$\ln RMW_{t-k}$	0.0293	0.0527	0.1169	0.3233
× $MATER_{t-k}$	(0.0500)	(0.0429)	(0.0822)	0.5637
	[0.0628]	[0.1130]	[0.2507]	
Interval	0.0007	0.0016	0.0441*	3.1422
	(0.0085)	(0.0024)	(0.0095)	0.4243
	[0.0011]	[0.0026]	[0.0158]	
R^2	0.95	0.95	0.94	N/A[c]
LM statistics	N/A	4.05	260.4	N/A

[a] Heteroskedasticity-resistant standard errors are in parentheses. Beta coefficients are in brackets. The mean of the dependent variable is 2.1886, with a standard deviation of 0.2628.

[b] * = significant at the 5% level.

[c] N/A = not applicable.

database; and a generalized least squares, random-effects model, with both group and period effects. The entries under these columns of Table 5.1 show the estimated coefficient, its heteroskedasticity-resistant standard error, and a beta coefficient for each independent variable. The beta coefficient measures the effect of a one-standard-deviation increase in the independent variable on the dependent variable, *ceteris paribus*, expressed as a fraction of the dependent variable's standard deviation. Thus, the beta coefficients can be used to compare the relative influence each independent variable has on the average real wage level. The rightmost column reports the mean (upper value) and standard deviation (lower value) for each variable.

The final row of Table 5.1 reports Lagrange multiplier (LM) statistics for the two GLS regressions, testing the random effects models versus the OLS model. The LM statistics favor both random-effects models over the OLS regression and favor them by a large margin in the case of the model incorporating both group and period random effects. Given the R^2 and LM results, the discussion will focus on the GLS regression with group and period effects.

The estimate of the coefficient on the lagged dependent variable in this regression, while indicating a high degree of persistence in the average real wage over time, does present evidence of an error-correction mechanism. The coefficient is statistically significant and less than 1, and its point estimate suggests that an increase in the log of the real wage in time period t would dissipate by about 20 percent, *ceteris paribus*, over the following k years. This finding is consistent with other findings that local labor markets do adjust to shocks in the manner suggested by basic theory, but that such adjustments occur over a long period (see Eberts and Stone 1992).

There is also evidence that the real wage in the local occupational labor markets under study responds as expected to short-run changes in the rate of occupational unemployment. The coefficients for the current change in the unemployment rate and for the unemployment rate lagged one year are both estimated to be negative, although only the coefficient for the latter variable is substantially greater than the corresponding standard error. Cyclical or structural factors that cause a one-point rise in the unemployment rate for a local occupational labor market would have a short-run effect within one year, lowering the average real wage by about 0.5 percent.

In a dynamic model such as this, the long-run response of the dependent variable Y to a given change in an independent variable X, holding other effects constant and taking into account the feedback from the lagged values of the dependent variable, is given by

Eq. 5.3 $\Delta Y = (\Delta X)[(\beta_1 + \beta_2)/(1 - \alpha)]$

where α, β_1, and β_2 are the coefficients defined in Eqs. 5.1 and 5.2. Because in this section Y is defined as the logarithm of the average real wage, the proportionate change in the real wage resulting from a given *ceteris paribus* change in an independent variable X is given by

Eq. 5.4 $\%\Delta(\text{Real Wage}) = (e^{\Delta Y} - 1)100$

Calculated in this way, the long-run effect of a permanent one-point increase in the unemployment rate would be to lower the average real wage by 1.9 percent. The long-run elasticity of the real wage in response to a 1 percent increase in the mean unemployment rate is –0.13, which is very similar to the results reported in the wage curve literature (Blanchflower and Oswald 1994).

The control variables for the skill mix of the specific jobs in an occupational group and those for the industry mix in the metropolitan area are positive and statistically significant. The real wage is higher in local occupational labor markets that have a higher proportion of workers in jobs that require higher skills and in markets where shifts in the job mix increase the relative proportion of jobs with higher skill requirements. The real wage is also higher in local occupational labor markets that have an industry mix more heavily weighted with industries estimated to have a high industry-specific compensation effect. Changes in the local industry mix away from high-compensation industries would result in a lower average occupational wage. Interestingly, the wage effect of changes in the industry mix would be just the opposite if we were to look solely at the OLS results (without group and period effects).

In all three regressions, union contract coverage also has a statistically significant positive effect on the real wage level for local occupational labor markets. For every one-point decrease in union contract coverage, the model predicts a long-run decrease in the average real wage of 0.35 percent, holding constant the effects of other variables. As Table 3.5 reported, on average, union contract coverage fell by 18 percentage points for plant workers and 2 points for office workers over the entire period sampled. These declines would translate into a 6.1 percent decrease in the real wage of maintenance and movement workers and a 0.7 percent decrease in the real wage of office-clerical and professional-technical workers.

For all four occupational groups, changes in the log of the real minimum wage (RMW) are positively correlated with the average wage level and are statistically significant. The short-run impact of a change in the minimum wage is felt most strongly in the market for material movement workers. Interestingly, the estimated coefficients for the lagged level of the real minimum wage are not statistically different from zero, even at the 10 percent significance level. This suggests that changes in the minimum wage have no long-run effect on the average real occupational wage rate.

The results are reassuring in that they support generally held views regarding the factors behind the sluggish growth of real wages in the United States during the period included in the database. High unemployment rates during the recessions of the 1980s had a negative effect on real wages, an effect only partially offset by longer-run market adjustments. The changing mix of skills within occupations, shifts in the mix of local industry away from high-wage industries, and the decline in union contract coverage and in the real minimum wage also contributed to changes in the local occupational real wage level. The beta coefficients offer one way to determine the relative effects of market and institutional forces on the real wage.

The beta coefficients shown in Table 5.1 are broadly similar for all the statistically significant independent variables with the exception of the lagged dependent variable and the lagged skill-mix measure. The estimated beta coefficient is −0.07 for the lagged unemployment rate, 0.05 for the change in industry mix, 0.03 for the lagged industry mix, 0.04 for the change in union contract coverage, 0.07 for the lagged union contract coverage rate, and 0.03 to 0.07 for the change in the log of the real minimum wage. The skill-mix variables have a strong effect on the dependent variable, with beta coefficients of 0.09 for the change in skill mix and 0.64 for the lagged level of the skill-mix measure. The beta coefficients suggest, then, that short-run labor-market forces, institutional changes in the minimum wage, and union contract coverage were about equally important in influencing changes in the average real wage from the mid 1970s to the beginning of the 1990s.

How well does the wage model explain the changes in relative wages noted in Chapter 2? One way to answer this question is to see how the model fits the situation in a given metropolitan area. Los Angeles serves as a case study.

The model has four variables that can account for movements in relative wage levels: 1) the occupational unemployment rate, 2) the occupational skill mix, 3) the collective bargaining coverage rate, and 4) the occupational-specific minimum wage effect. The other independent variables have common effects on all four occupational groups. The unemployment rate for all four occupational groups in Los Angeles rose from 1978 to 1984, in response to the serious recessions of the early 1980s, and fell from 1984 to 1989 as the economy recovered. However, the recessionary effects were much milder and the expansionary effects much stronger for the two white-collar groups. The unemployment rate of laborers relative to clerical workers was 1.88 in 1978 and 2.4 in 1989, and the ratio of the laborers' rate to that for professional-technical workers rose from 2.4 in 1978 to 5.5 in 1989. The unemployment rates for the two blue-collar groups maintained roughly the same relative relationship throughout the period.

From 1978 to 1989, the skill mix in Los Angeles generally rose for office-clerical and professional-technical workers, fell slightly for skilled maintenance workers, and remained largely unchanged for material movement workers. Union contract coverage fell from 18 percent to 12 percent for white-collar workers and from 59 percent to 48 percent for blue-collar workers over the same period. Finally, the real minimum wage in Los Angeles fell by 30 percent from 1978 to 1989. Given the regression estimates in Table 5.1, all three factors would be expected to widen the relative wage gap between white-collar and blue-collar workers.

The changes in the independent variables are consistent with the changes in the relative occupational wage levels shown in Figure 5.1. Relative wage measures were constructed by dividing the actual wage and the wage predicted by the GLS model (with group and period effects for office-clerical, professional-technical, and skilled maintenance workers) by the actual and the predicted wage levels for material movement workers. Relative wages rose the most for professional-technical workers and rose slightly for office-clerical workers, while relative wages for skilled maintenance jobs remained unchanged from 1978 to 1984 and rose slightly thereafter. Figure 5.1 also suggests that

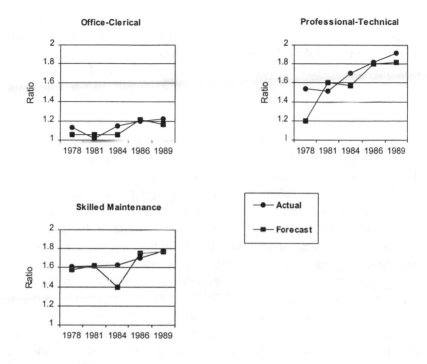

Figure 5.1 Ratio of Wages Relative to Material Movement Worker Wages, Los Angeles

the GLS wage regression matched the changes in relative wages in Los Angeles from 1978 to 1989. The correlation between the actual relative wage and that derived from the wage levels predicted by the model for the 15 observations available for Los Angeles is 0.97. For Los Angeles, then, differences across occupations in the strength of labor demand relative to labor supply, in changes in the skill mix of jobs, in changes in union influence, and in the minimum wage help to account for the widening of relative wage levels during the 1980s.

AN ANALYSIS OF THE VARIANCE OF REAL WAGES

The second factor contributing to the rise in overall wage inequality in the 20 metropolitan areas in the 1980s was an increase in the variance of the hourly wages paid within each of the four occupational groups. Table 5.2 gives estimates of the determinants of the variance of the logarithm of real wages in local occupational labor markets. Like the real wage level regressions discussed above, these estimates are based on 364 observations of 80 local occupational labor markets over time. Unlike the real wage regressions, the Lagrange multiplier statistics (Table 5.2, last row) reject the two GLS random-effects models in favor of the OLS regression. Because of this result and because the estimated coefficients are very similar for all three regressions, the discussion here will focus on the OLS regression.

The estimated coefficients for the lagged dependent variable provide evidence of an error-correction mechanism, with the coefficient statistically significant and less than 1. An increase in the wage variance within an occupation in period t would be dissipated by about 20 percent during the next k years. The wage variance exhibits about the same persistence as the average occupational wage level. On the other hand, the wage variance appears to be more responsive to short-run changes in the occupational unemployment rate than the average occupational wage level. A one-point increase in the occupational unemployment rate would raise the wage variance within that occupational group by 9 percent, which is substantially greater than the response of the average wage to unemployment discussed above.[1] This suggests that the wage response to cyclical or structural unemployment is substantially greater throughout the wage distribution than perhaps is reflected in changes in the mean wage level.

The estimated response of the wage variance to the unemployment rate is of interest because several economists have found little evidence for a cyclical component to the national rise in wage inequality during the 1980s (Gottschalk 1997). However, previous studies by Katz and Revenga (1989) and Karoly and Klerman (1994) estimated statistically significant positive relationships between inequality measures and local or regional rates of unemployment. Bartik (1994, 1996) concluded that an acceleration of employment growth in a metropolitan area has its greatest effect on the wages of the poorest workers.

The change in the skill mix of jobs and in the lagged level of the skill mix are both statistically significant and negatively related to the wage variance within occupations. Wage rates show less inequality in local occupational labor markets that have a higher concentration

Table 5.2   Determinants of the Variance of the Real Wage[a]

Variable	OLS	GLS (group)	GLS (group & time)	Mean, std. dev.
Constant	7.0075*[b]	7.1929*	6.8955*	—
	(1.9776)	(1.8547)	(2.1111)	
Variance$_{t-k}$	0.8216*	0.8025*	0.8082*	9.1316
	(0.0359)	(0.0271)	(0.0277)	5.4874
	[0.7942]	[0.7757]	[0.7812]	
Δ% Unemployed$_t$	0.0778*	0.0771*	0.0542	−0.2679
	(0.0359)	(0.0329)	(0.0366)	2.8442
	[0.0389]	[0.0386]	[0.0271]	
% Unemployed$_{t-1}$	0.2114*	0.2159*	0.1576*	6.8923
	(0.0053)	(0.0309)	(0.0360)	4.8850
	[0.1819]	[0.1858]	[0.1356]	
Δln(Skill)$_t$	−4.8722*	−4.9094*	−4.2443*	−0.0048
	(1.1692)	(1.0628)	(1.1098)	0.0824
	[−0.0707]	[−0.0712]	[−0.0616]	
ln(Skill)$_{t-k}$	−0.9896*	−1.0457*	−1.4886*	2.6208
	(0.2574)	(0.2435)	(0.2685)	1.0556
	[−0.1840]	[−0.1944]	[−0.2768]	
ΔIndustry mix$_t$	0.1847*	0.1790*	0.0991	−0.3462
	(0.0816)	(0.0745)	(0.0934)	1.2068
	[0.0392]	[0.0380]	[0.0211]	
Industry mix$_{t-k}$	0.0705	0.0736	−0.0010	6.0973
	(0.0582)	(0.0562)	(0.0644)	1.6639
	[0.0207]	[0.0216]	[−0.0003]	
ΔUnion$_t$	−0.0016	−0.0033	−0.0025	−2.1819
	(0.0209)	(0.0189)	(0.0185)	4.8302
	[−0.0014]	[−0.0028]	[−0.0021]	
Union$_{t-k}$	−0.0115*	−0.0117*	−0.0133*	33.6500
	(0.0053)	(0.0051)	(0.0054)	26.3625
	[−0.0534]	[−0.0543]	[−0.0618]	
ΔRelative minimum$_t$	−4.6860	−4.5674	0.2854	−0.0193
	(2.5512)	(2.3196)	(3.4124)	0.0398
	[−0.0328]	[−0.0320]	[0.0020]	

(continued)

Table 5.2   (continued)

Variable	OLS	GLS (group)	GLS (group & time)	Mean, std. dev.
Relative minimum$_{t-k}$	−5.8197*	−5.7052*	−9.7077*	0.4168
	(1.8212)	(1.7168)	(2.0326)	0.1073
	[−0.1100]	[−0.1078]	[−0.1835]	
Interval	−0.3770	−0.3633	0.8807*	3.1422
	(0.2363)	(0.2170)	(0.3024)	0.4243
	[−0.0282]	[−0.0271]	[0.0658]	
R^2	0.91	0.91	0.90	N/A[c]
LM statistics	N/A	1.81	4.64	N/A

[a] Heteroskedasticity-resistant standard errors are in parentheses. Beta coefficients are in brackets. The current and lagged values of the variance are multiplied by 100. The mean of the dependent variable is 9.8211, with a standard deviation of 5.6766.
[b] * = significant at the 5% level.
[c] N/A = not applicable.

of more highly skilled jobs and in markets where the job mix is shifting toward more highly skilled jobs. Skill mix has, then, two potentially offsetting effects on the wage distribution: it serves to raise average wages and (as we saw in the case of Los Angeles) it adds to changes in relative wages across occupations, but at the same time it acts to reduce wage inequality within local occupational labor markets.[2]

The coefficient for the lagged level of the industry mix is not statistically significant from zero in the regressions, although changes in the industry mix toward higher-paying industries is positively correlated with wage inequality within local occupational labor markets. The result presumably reflects an increase in the wage level for those working in high-wage sectors relative to that of workers in the same occupation but employed in low-wage industries. As the focus is on wage inequality <u>within</u> occupations, the shift away from manufacturing and other high-wage industries toward the service sector is seen as <u>reducing</u> wage disparities among similar workers.

The lagged level of the union variable is statistically significant and negatively correlated with the wage variance in local occupational labor markets. Changes in the rate of union coverage do not have a statistically significant effect on the wage variance in the regressions reported in Table 5.2. As has been found in a number of previous empirical studies, wages are more equally distributed among similar workers in the more heavily unionized local labor markets. The regression estimates indicate that a decrease of one percentage point in the rate of union contract coverage, *ceteris paribus*, would lead to a 0.7 percent increase in within-group wage inequality. Like the result for the unemployment rate, it appears that the wage variance is substantially more sensitive to changes in union coverage than is the average wage level.

In the regressions reported in Table 5.2, the minimum wage effect is measured by the locally relevant minimum wage divided by the average wage in the local occupational labor market. This measure suggests that the minimum wage is more important in labor markets where the gap between the minimum and the average wage is smallest. Both the lagged level and the change in this relative minimum wage variable are statistically significant and negatively correlated with the occupational wage variance. An increase in the relative minimum wage raises the wage floor and thus reduces the range of wage rates and wage disparity. The results suggest that the relative minimum wage has a fairly large impact on the wage variance within local occupational labor markets. A 10-point increase in the relative minimum wage, *ceteris paribus*, would be associated with a 9.8 percent short-run decrease and a 33 percent long-run decrease in the wage variance relative to its mean value.

The high degree of explanatory power shown by the wage variance regressions and the empirical support the regressions provide for generally accepted explanations of rising wage inequality are reassuring. The estimated coefficients suggest that increased wage inequality within occupations reflects high unemployment during the first half of the 1980s and the decline in the extent of union contract coverage and in the relative minimum wage during that decade. These inequality-increasing forces would have been offset to some extent by an increase in the skill mix within an occupation and by a shift away from high-compensation industries.

The beta coefficients offer some insight into the relative importance of market and institutional factors in explaining changes in the wage variance within local occupational labor markets. The evidence

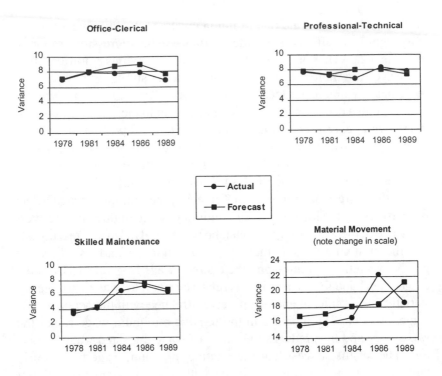

Figure 5.2 Variances of the log of Real Wages, Los Angeles

again suggests that both forces were important, although here the balance shifts somewhat toward short-run market factors. The beta coefficients are –0.04 for the change in the unemployment rate and –0.18 for the lagged unemployment rate. For the institutional variables, the beta coefficients are –0.05 for the lagged union contract coverage rate, –0.03 for the change in the relative minimum wage, and –0.11 for the lagged relative minimum wage.

By looking at the relationship between the actual and fitted values of the variance for each of the four groups in Los Angeles, we can check the ability of the OLS regression to account for changes in the wage variance. The actual and fitted values are plotted in Figure 5.2. There is a fairly close fit between the actual data and the variances predicted by the model, with the correlation between the two variables at 0.95 for the 20 observations for Los Angeles.

Keep in mind when assessing the time series patterns in Figure 5.2 that California raised its minimum wage from $3.35 to $4.25 in 1989 (Neumark and Wascher 1992), leading to a corresponding rise in the relative minimum wage for all four occupational groups. For example, after falling by about 29 percent from 1978 to 1986, the relative minimum wage for office-clerical workers rose by 17 percent between 1986 and 1989. This rise in the relative minimum wage reinforced the effects of falling occupational unemployment and contributed to the observed decrease in wage variance in the four occupational labor markets in Los Angeles at the end of the 1980s. The change in the relative minimum wage alone could account for about 17.5 percent of the decrease in the wage variance for office-clerical workers in Los Angeles between 1986 and 1989.

AN ANALYSIS OF THE 50–25 WAGE DIFFERENTIAL

Since we are interested in the way changes in the wage structure have affected the lowest-paid workers, the wage model was also estimated with the difference between the logarithm of hourly wages for workers at the 50th and 25th percentiles of the occupational wage distribution as the dependent variable. The results are found in Table 5.3. With the R^2 statistic at 0.74, this application of the model has slightly less explanatory power than the real wage and wage variance versions discussed above. Like the wage variance model, the Lagrange multiplier statistics reject both GLS random-effects models in favor of the OLS model. Apparently, group and period effects beyond those captured in the independent variables are not important determinants of the variance and the 50–25 differential.

The estimated coefficients for the lagged 50–25 differential show the lowest degree of persistence and the highest error-correction response of the three sets of regressions discussed in this chapter. Some 40 percent of an increase in the 50–25 differential in period t would be eliminated by medium-term labor market adjustments in the following k years.

The occupational unemployment rate lagged one year has a statistically significant positive correlation with the 50–25 wage differ-

Table 5.3   Determinants of the 50–25 Percentile Wage Differential[a]

Variable	OLS	GLS (group)	GLS (group & time)	Mean, std. dev.
Constant	40.6280*[b]	57.8070*	44.7830*	—
	(7.1139)	(4.1067)	(8.2169)	
50–25 Differential$_{t-k}$	0.6003*	0.5781*	0.5707*	23.4345
	(0.0418)	(0.0411)	(0.0425)	11.8310
	[0.5799]	[0.5585]	[0.5513]	
Δ% Unemployed$_t$	−0.1112	−0.1001	−0.0977	−0.2679
	(0.1359)	(0.1309)	(0.1506)	2.8442
	[−0.0258]	[−0.0232]	[−0.0227]	
% Unemployed$_{t-1}$	0.6025*	0.6165*	0.6104*	6.8923
	(0.1271)	(0.1229)	(0.1460)	4.8850
	[0.2403]	[0.2459]	[0.2434]	
Δln(Skill)$_t$	−7.4279	−7.4909	−7.8405	−0.0048
	(4.4227)	(4.2310)	(4.5801)	0.0824
	[−0.0499]	[−0.0504]	[−0.0527]	
ln(Skill)$_{t-k}$	−4.6265*	−4.7902*	−5.6458*	2.6208
	(0.8805)	(0.8651)	(1.0021)	1.0556
	[−0.3988]	[−0.4129]	[−0.4867]	
ΔIndustry mix$_t$	0.5344	0.5251	0.1713	−0.3462
	(0.3082)	(0.2958)	(0.3815)	1.2068
	[0.0527]	[0.0517]	[0.0168]	
Industry mix$_{t-k}$	0.1608	0.1624	−0.2218	6.0973
	(0.2194)	(0.2206)	(0.2529)	1.6639
	[0.0218]	[0.0221]	[−0.0301]	
ΔUnion$_t$	−0.0069	−0.0008	−0.0016	−2.1819
	(0.0770)	(0.0741)	(0.0770)	4.8302
	[−0.0027]	[−0.0003]	[−0.0006]	
Union$_{t-k}$	−0.0332	−0.0335	−0.0466*	33.6500
	(0.0184)	(0.0198)	(0.0213)	26.3625
	[−0.0715]	[−0.0721]	[−0.1003]	
ΔRelative minimum$_t$	−27.1350*	−26.7830*	−32.0320*	−0.0193
	(9.6388)	(9.2165)	(13.7620)	0.0398
	[−0.0882]	[−0.0870]	[−0.1041]	

Table 5.3   (continued)

Variable	OLS	GLS (group)	GLS (group & time)	Mean, std. dev.
Relative minimum$_{t-k}$	−37.0410*	−37.470*	−46.2290*	0.4168
	(6.8580)	(6.7419)	(8.1462)	0.1073
	[−0.3245]	[−0.3283]	[−0.4050]	
Interval	−2.1991*	−2.2220*	−0.5398	3.1422
	(0.8954)	(0.8640)	(1.2125)	0.4243
	[−0.0762]	[−0.0769]	[−0.0187]	
R^2	0.74	0.74	0.72	N/A^c
LM statistic	N/A	1.52	2.06	N/A

[a] Heteroskedasticity-resistant standard errors in parentheses. Beta coefficients are in brackets. The current and lagged values of the dependent variable are multiplied by 100. The mean of the dependent variable is 24.5748, with a standard deviation of 12.2460.
[b] * = significant at the 5% level.
[c] N/A = not applicable.

ential in local occupational labor markets. The estimated effect on the dependent variable of a change in the rate in the current year is substantially less than its estimated standard error in all three regressions in Table 5.3. The 50–25 wage differential exhibits a fairly strong response to the lagged unemployment rate: a one-point increase would raise the mean wage differential in the short run by about 2 percent. The long-run effect of a permanent one-point increase in the unemployment rate is estimated to be a 6.2 percent increase in the mean 50–25 wage differential in the sample. Again, there is evidence that short-run cyclical or structural changes in the rate of unemployment within an occupation have a greater impact on the wage distribution— particularly at the low-wage end of the distribution—than on the average wage level.

As with the wage variance results, changes in the skill mix and in the lagged level of that mix within an occupation have a statistically significant negative correlation with the wage differential between the 50th and 25th percentiles in the local occupational wage distribution. The statistically significant positive coefficient estimated for the change in the industry-mix variable also reinforces the wage variance results. A shift away from high-compensation industries works to reduce wage inequality within an occupation by lowering the differential between the worker at the 50th and the worker at the 25th percentile.

The change effect is not statistically significant for either institutional variable. However, the lagged rate for union contract coverage has a statistically significant negative effect on the 50–25 differential. Evaluated at the means of the data, the 18-point average drop in union coverage for plant workers would raise the 50–25 wage differential by 8.5 percent. This is added evidence that unionization works to equalize the wage distribution by reducing the relative disadvantage of the lowest paid workers.

As suggested by the non-parametric evidence of DiNardo and Lemieux (1997), the minimum wage is very important in determining of the shape of the wage distribution below the median. A relative minimum wage that was permanently 10 percent higher would eventually lower the 50–25 gap by 17.5 percent. The importance of the minimum wage is also reflected in the beta coefficients. In the OLS regression, the beta coefficients are 0.24 for the lagged unemployment rate, –0.05 for the change in the occupational skill mix, –0.40 for the lagged skill mix, –0.07 for lagged union contract coverage, and –0.32 for the lagged relative minimum wage. Skill mix is also important in determining the 50–25 differential, but the relative minimum wage has slightly greater influence on the dependent variable than does the occupational unemployment rate and substantially greater influence than does the rate of union contract coverage.

OVERALL WAGE INEQUALITY

The analysis in this chapter began with the observation that changes over time in the variance of wages for all workers could be decomposed into changes in the variance within occupations and changes in the relative wage across occupations. That was the reason for the separate analyses of the determinants of the logarithm of the average real wage and of the variance of the real wage in local occu-

pational labor markets. Now the analysis turns to the regression results
to see how well the forecasts from the wage structure model fit the
data for the overall wage distribution for all workers.

The variance decomposition formula used in Chapter 2 to examine the relative contribution of changes in wage inequality between
and within occupations for overall changes in urban wage inequality
is reproduced as Equation 5.5:

Eq. 5.5 $$\sigma_t^2 = \sum_i p_{it} \, \sigma_{it}^2 + \sum_i p_{it} \, (W_{it} - W_t)^2$$

where p_i is the fraction of workers in occupation i for a given metropolitan area, σ_i^2 is the wage variance within occupation i, W_{it} is the logarithm of the average real hourly wage in occupation i for period t, and
W_t is the logarithm of the average real hourly wage for all workers in
that area. The equation can be used to forecast the wage variance for
all workers from forecast values of the wage variance within occupations and the average occupational real wage. The fitted values from
the OLS regression in Table 5.2 and the GLS regression with group and
time effects in Table 5.1 are used for those forecasts.

Table 5.4 presents data on the overall variance and the forecast
overall variance for all workers, derived from the fitted values from
the occupational real wage and wage variance regressions. The entries
in Table 5.4 are for the initial and final years for each metropolitan
area in the regressions. In general, the forecasts derived from the separate occupational real wage and wage variance regressions are rea-
sonably accurate. For both periods, the means of the actual and the
forecast values are very similar, the mean absolute errors and the mean
squared errors are small relative to the mean actual and forecast values, and the actual and fitted values are closely correlated among the
20 labor markets.

The accuracy of the overall wage variance forecasts in Table 5.4
suggests that the models in this chapter do capture the main determinants of the changes in relative real wages across occupations and that
they also capture the variance of wages within the occupations in the
sample. These results, plus the evidence for Los Angeles, also suggest that estimating a common model for all four occupations and all
20 metropolitan areas does not seriously distort the estimated impact

Table 5.4   The Actual and the Forecast Values of the Wage Variance for All Workers

Metropolitan area	Year	Actual	Forecast[a]	Year	Actual	Forecast[a]
Anaheim	1978	0.1387	0.1393	1988	0.1571	0.1541
Atlanta	1978	0.1717	0.1411	1991	0.2003	0.1911
Baltimore	1978	0.1784	0.1760	1991	0.2024	0.2382
Chicago	1977	0.1157	0.1177	1986	0.1550	0.1699
Cincinnati	1977	0.1433	0.1360	1989	0.1889	0.1928
Cleveland	1977	0.1409	0.1430	1990	0.2379	0.1906
Detroit	1979	0.1005	0.1461	1989	0.1993	0.1893
Houston	1977	0.1755	0.1539	1990	0.3113	0.2380
Indianapolis	1978	0.1731	0.1657	1988	0.2165	0.2156
Los Angeles	1978	0.1342	0.1400	1989	0.1808	0.1938
Miami	1978	0.1300	0.1326	1990	0.1821	0.2080
Milwaukee	1978	0.1450	0.1345	1991	0.1907	0.2388
Minneapolis	1978	0.1331	0.1202	1991	0.1607	0.1600
Nassau–Suffolk	1978	0.1334	0.1273	1987	0.1411	0.1653
New York	1978	0.1089	0.1204	1988	0.1649	0.2061
Philadelphia	1979	0.1544	0.1342	1988	0.1787	0.1985
San Diego	1977	0.1270	0.1247	1989	0.2001	0.2162
San Jose	1978	0.1142	0.1023	1988	0.1520	0.1429
Seattle	1977	0.1230	0.1174	1988	0.1718	0.1807
St. Louis	1979	0.1631	0.1502	1989	0.2370	0.2229
Mean		0.1400	0.1361		0.1914	0.1956
Mean absolute error		0.0113			0.0209	
Mean squared error		0.0002			0.0008	
Correlation coefficient		0.7406			0.6805	

[a] Forecast values are the author's estimates, based on forecasts from the real wage and the wage variance regressions discussed in Chapter 5. See the text for details.

of these determinants on the occupational real wage level or on the real wage variance.

SUMMARY

This chapter has presented an analysis of the determinants of changing wage inequality in 20 local labor markets. A general dynamic model was applied to a panel data set with 364 observations on four occupational groups in 20 areas at selected intervals from 1974 to 1991. Because changes in wage inequality reflect both changes in the relative wage across occupations and changes in wage inequality within occupations, and because of particular concern for the relative position of the lowest wage earners, the model was estimated separately with the log of the real wage, the variance of the log of the real wage, and the log wage differential between the 50th and 25th percentiles as the dependent variables. This analysis paid particular attention to examining the relative importance of market and institutional factors.

The wage structure responds to short-run shifts in the labor market, as measured by the local rate of unemployment within an occupation, and to longer-run market adjustments as measured by the error-correction mechanism in the model. Short-run changes in unemployment rate had a greater estimated effect on the wage variance (and in particular on the 50–25 wage differential) than on the average occupational real wage level. The real wage level also showed more long-run persistence than did either distribution measure. Close to half of a shock to the 50–25 differential would be dissipated over the following three years. In addition to its usefulness in explaining changes in wage inequality in metropolitan labor markets, the finding of higher unemployment at the margins of the wage distribution could help to clarify how the wage structure responds to cyclical and structural changes in unemployment.

The most closely studied institutional factors in the literature on wage inequality are the changes in the relative importance of collective bargaining and changes in the minimum wage. Our results indicate that both were statistically important in explaining changes in the level and distribution of wages in the sample. Markets with a higher percentage of workers in firms where union contracts covered a majority of workers had higher real wage levels, a lower wage variance, and a smaller 50–25 wage differential. Increases in the real minimum wage were reflected in higher average wage levels for an occupation, especially for material movement workers. Local markets with a higher minimum wage relative to the average wage registered significantly lower wage variances and 50–25 differentials. The beta coefficients suggest that the market and institutions had equal influence on the real wage, although market factors may be slightly more important in explaining changes in the wage variance. As might be expected, the relative minimum wage was a very important determinant of the 50–25 wage differential.

Two variables introduced to control for composition effects gave interesting results. The control variable for changes in the job mix within occupations was the weighted average of the months of specific preparation required for jobs. This variable was statistically significant and empirically important in all of the regressions. Those local occupational labor markets with high-skill job mixes or with job mixes changing toward jobs with higher skill requirements had higher average wages and more equally distributed wages. The second control variable, for changes in the industry mix of firms surveyed in the AWS, was the weighted average of an estimate of the industry-specific compensation effect. This variable was less important in the regressions, perhaps because the AWS data identified industries only by very broad aggregates, or perhaps because the effect of changes in the industry mix are reflected in unemployment rates (Hyclak 1996).

On the basis of the analysis in this chapter, the rise in urban wage inequality during the 1980s can be explained as reflecting a widening of the gap between the relative wages across occupations and as reflecting a rise in wage inequality within occupations. A key factor is the greater cyclical impact of the deep recessions of the early 1980s on blue-collar workers. Rising relative wage inequality would be due to this difference in the unemployment response, exacerbated by the persistence of high real wages, by declining union contract coverage, and by differences across occupations in the skill-related job mix. The fall in the real minimum wage had a particularly pronounced impact on the average real wage for material movement workers. Rising wage inequality within occupations would be due to the higher rates of unemployment during the 1980s, falling union contract coverage rates, and a falling relative minimum wage rate. In the office-clerical and professional-technical occupations, rising average skill levels would have moderated the tendency toward greater within-occupation inequality. The separate models for the occupational real wage and for real wage variance generate forecast values that accurately portray changes over time in the wage variance for all workers in the sample.

During the early 1980s, unemployment rates rose markedly for all workers. By the end of the decade, the unemployment rates for blue-collar workers had generally increased relative to those for the white-collar workers in the sample. Given our result that the changes in wage inequality were responsive both to short-run labor market shocks and to longer-run market adjustments, the extent to which changes in labor market reflect permanent changes in "natural" levels or are more fleeting responses to cyclical or structural forces remains an important question. Clearly, much of the literature that cites technological change and changes in international trade as explanations for changes in the wage structure suggest that these changes are indeed permanent. At the same time, we must remember that the 1980s, especially the early years of that decade, were years of unusually high labor market stress in many localities.

Notes

1. With the regression results for the wage variance and the 50–25 wage differential, we calculate the percentage change in the dependent variable for a given change in an independent variable as $(\Delta Y/\overline{Y})100$, where ΔY is given by Eq. 5.3.
2. It is important to note that this discussion refers to the *ceteris paribus* effect of changes in the job mix of the four occupational groups. Changes in the occupational unemployment rates might also reflect changes in the demand for various skills. In general, the unemployment rates of the two blue-collar groups in the sample rose in comparison with the rates of the white-collar group over the sample period. This would lead to a rise in overall inequality within and across occupational groups.

6 Summary and Policy Implications

SUMMARY OF THE RESULTS

Chapter 1 posed five questions about wage inequality. The answers to those questions summarize the results from this study of 20 metropolitan labor markets.

1. Are trends in the structure of wages in local labor markets similar to the trends in the structure of wages as revealed in nationwide data sets?

The short answer is yes. Chapter 2 reveals broad similarities between the trend toward greater wage inequality, revealed by studies of national samples of workers such as the CPS, and the trend toward greater wage inequality found in local samples such as the AWS. This finding is important for two reasons. First, and most important, it suggests that the rise in wage incquality in the United States during the 1980s reflected, in part, a significant change in the structure of the real hourly wages for specific occupations and was not solely a reflection of changes in the demographic characteristics of workers or in the stability of their employment. Second, the rise in wage inequality within each of the 20 metropolitan labor markets in the sample suggests that the rise in wage inequality seen in national samples was indeed widespread and not due mainly to the substantial regional shifts in population and economic activity that took place during the period.

2. Do local labor markets differ in the extent and pattern of the rise in wage inequality?

Significant differences did appear. For several metropolitan areas, the variance of the logarithm of the real hourly wage fell at the end of the sample period, after rising steadily for several years. Metropolitan areas differed in the extent to which the rise in wage inequality reflected a rise in the 50–25 wage differential or in the 75–50 wage differential. In several cases, the data suggest that rising inequality stemmed largely from rising wage differentials among workers earning more than the median wage; in others, wage inequality rose mainly among workers earning less than the median. There were also inter-area differences in the relative importance of sources of wage inequality between and within occupations and in the pattern of trends in inequality for the four occupational groups. The study used the considerable cross-section differences in the sample to test general hypotheses about the causes of the rise in wage inequality.

3.   Have changes in the availability of benefits accompanied changes in the wage structure?

The AWS reported the prevalence of various benefits offered to plant and office workers. The analysis of that data (see Chapter 3) suggests two main conclusions. First, the evidence for office-clerical workers shows a rise in the amount of time off for holidays and vacations and a rise in the percentage of workers receiving various benefits. Second, the results for plant workers are more mixed, but it appears that the availability of benefits was stable or falling in most metropolitan areas. These results point to a rise in the relative availability of benefits for office workers.

4.   How have the wage returns on skills changed over time?

Chapter 4 examined the changing role of skill requirements in determining the average hourly wage for specific job titles among the 16 labor markets in the sample for which data are available for both the late 1970s and late 1980s. Skill requirements were measured by variables drawn from the *Dictionary of Occupational Titles* and by the index of the job level in the AWS. A comparison of the results for the late 1970s and late 1980s shows a rise in the wage return on the highest skill levels for specific vocational preparation, general educational development related to language skills, and the skills represented by the index of the job level. By way of contrast, the wage advantage for workers in jobs requiring higher machine-related job skills appears to have fallen between the late 1970s and late 1980s.

The results support the conclusion in the literature that higher returns on skills—in particular cognitive skill—played an important role in widening the wage gap between workers holding jobs requiring different levels of skill.

5. What is the relative importance of changes in union contract coverage and in the minimum wage in explaining changes in the wage structure?

Chapter 5 set out a model designed to explain changes in the wage structure across 20 local labor markets from 1974 to 1991. Because the overall changes seen in the sample could be traced both to changes in the relative wage across occupations and to changes in the wage distribution within occupations, the models in Chapter 5 were used for separate analyses of the roles of market and institutional factors in shaping the changes. In addition to studying the correlates of the variance in wage rates within occupations, the analysis also focused on the factors related to changes in the wage differential between the 50th and 25th percentiles of the wage distribution within occupations.

The results of the analysis in Chapter 5 indicate that both market and institutional factors were significantly related to all three measures of the local wage structure. The estimated impact of union contract coverage and of the minimum wage on the dependent variables was equivalent to that of the local occupational unemployment rate. Local occupational labor markets with greater union influence and a higher minimum wage had a higher average real wage, a smaller wage variance, and a smaller differential between the median wage and the wage at the 25th percentile of the distribution. Higher local occupational unemployment rates were associated with lower average real wages and with a more widely dispersed wage distribution. And shifts in the job mix toward jobs with higher skill requirements also boosted the average wage level and reduced wage inequality.

The predicted real wage level and the predicted wage variance for each local labor market were used to calculate the predicted overall wage variance for the initial and final years for each market in the sample. The predicted wage variance was very close to the mark for all 20 areas, and the prediction error was small across the 20 areas for both periods, suggesting that the models captured the primary determinants of changes in the local wage structure and that the use of a single model encompassing all four occupations did not seriously distort the estimated parameters. While the results say something about the relative importance of market and institutional factors in explaining changes over time and among areas, the results do not clarify the relative importance of trade and technology in driving shifts in the demand for labor.

POLICY IMPLICATIONS

Although many studies have sought to explain the rise in wage inequality in the United States during the 1980s, relatively few have made specific policy recommendations. Summers (1996) pointed out that no study has gone beyond the conclusion that the existing inequalities are "too great" and set out the social consequences of different degrees of wage inequality. And, as is suggested by the controversy surrounding Card and Krueger (1996), we lack a clear understanding of the equity-efficiency trade-offs implied by redistributive programs such as the minimum wage. The literature discusses several policies for reducing wage inequality (see Katz 1996). The results reported here touch on a few of those policies.

Macroeconomic Policy

A macroeconomic policy leading to sustained low unemployment rates is seen as one way of stimulating the demand for low-skilled workers and, through the type of hysteresis effects described by Bartik (1991) and others, improve their lifetime earnings. The research reported here finds that wage inequality shows a strong positive response to the unemployment rate in the local labor market and points to the possibility of a significant intermediate-run error-correction adjustment to past rises in inequality. This plus the evidence of recent reductions in wage inequality as measured by national indicators, traceable to good macroeconomic performance in recent years (Uchitelle 1997), lends considerable support to the argument that macroeconomic policy has an important role to play in improving wage equality.

Education and Training

Improved education and training are seen as a way of reducing the supply of workers for low-skill labor markets and of raising the supply of workers for high-skill markets (Levy 1995). Like many other studies, the research reported here shows that the wage advantage for workers in jobs requiring higher skills has risen over time, and that shifts in the composition of occupations toward jobs requiring higher skills has a significant equalizing effect on the wage distribution within occupations. This can be taken as evidence of shortages in the markets for skilled workers and would support a call for more education and training. One potentially disturbing finding from this study, however, is that the wage advantage for machine-related skills, typically associated with the most-skilled blue-collar jobs, seems to have fallen over time. If this should be corroborated by further research, it would call into question whether educational policies designed to teach such skills do significantly reduce wage inequality.

Raising the Minimum Wage

There is considerable agreement among economists with the analysis presented in the *1997 Economic Report of the President* on the equalizing effect of the minimum wage on the distribution of wages, particularly its effect in improving the relative wages of the poorest wage earners. The results reported here also support those conclusions. The minimum wage was negatively correlated with the variance of hourly real wages and with the 50–25 hourly wage differential over time for the sample of local occupational labor markets. Given the growing evidence that an unchanging nominal minimum wage contributed significantly to the rise in U.S. wage inequality during the 1980s and given the strong political opposition to raising the minimum wage because of its potentially adverse consequences for employment, it would appear imperative that labor economists attempt to more carefully quantify the equity and efficiency implications of changing the minimum wage.

Strengthening Collective Bargaining

A number of economists argue that the decline in union membership is an important determinant of wage inequality and that any significant policy action to reduce inequality should include measures to strengthen the role of collective bargaining in the setting of wages (Freeman 1997). The results reported here show collective bargaining coverage to have had an important effect in limiting the wage differential between workers at the 50th and the 25th percentiles of the wage distribution and in reducing wage inequality within occupations. However, there appears to be little support for the changes in labor law deemed necessary to restore collective bargaining to the levels seen in the past. On the contrary, most serious discussions of labor law reform envision changes in legislation that would promote a more cooperative labor relations climate than that embodied in the amended Wagner Act of 1935 (Block, Beck, and Kruger 1996). We have no data about the potential impact of cooperative labor-management relations on the distribution of wages.

Micro Demand Policy

The studies in the volume edited by Freeman and Gottschalk (1998) examined the efficacy of various policies designed to increase the demand for less-skilled workers. There is some evidence that wage subsidies can stimulate an increase in the employment opportunities for and raise the wage levels of less-skilled workers. The experience with such programs in the United States, however, indicates that the effects are likely to be modest. Direct public employment also adds to the demand for low-skilled labor, but questions remain about the long-run effects of such programs on their "graduates." Providing subsidies to influence the location of firms is very costly relative to the number of jobs created, and the benefits of such programs often accrue to nontargeted members of the population. All such programs face the criticism that transfer payments are more effective than subsidies in dealing with the effects of poverty. The experience with such programs in periods of greater governmental intervention in the labor market are also not very encouraging. Most programs have been short-lived experiments that ended prematurely.

Controlling Immigration

Briggs (1996) argued strongly that the immigration laws should be amended to limit the number of immigrants allowed to enter the United

States each year and to give preference to those with higher skills. Among other benefits, he saw such a policy as reducing the pressure of increased supply on low-wage labor markets. While one might expect high rates of immigration to be reflected in local unemployment rates, particularly for low-skilled workers, our study provides no direct evidence on this issue, and there is little evidence in the literature to support this conclusion (Borjas, Freeman, and Katz 1996, 1997). However, given the large influx of immigrants in recent years and their heavy concentration in a few areas (Clark 1996), the impact of immigration warrants continued research.

SUMMARY

There are three potentially important contributions from this project. First, changes in the wage distribution reflect, in part, changes in the structure of the real wages for specific jobs in local occupational labor markets. Second, the wage advantage for workers in the most-skilled jobs has risen over time, but the wage response to different aspects of skill is more complex than is typically seen in human capital models, where skill means only educational attainment and years of potential work experience. Third, changes in the distribution of wages within local labor markets appear to be very responsive in the short run to changes in local occupational unemployment rates. The wage distribution's responsiveness to market forces also appears to extend to the intermediate run and to embody a partial self-correction mechanism that might reflect changes in labor supply and demand in response to an initial rise or fall in wage disparities. The possibility that the sharp rise in U.S. wage inequality during the 1980s may have been caused in part by the deep recessions in the early years of that decade and might be partially self-correcting deserves further investigation.

7 Addendum:
Atlanta in 1991 and 1996

The end of the Area Wage Survey program in 1991 makes it impossible to extend the analysis to the 1990s. Partial information is available, however, for assessing whether the emergence of tight labor markets during the 1990s has acted to brake the rise in wage inequality. Atlanta serves as a case study of changes in wage inequality from 1991 to 1996.

The Occupational Compensation Survey (which replaced the Area Wage Survey) continued to report wage distribution data for 20 of the job titles used in our study, including four from the professional-technical group, five from the office-clerical group, five from the skilled maintenance group, and six from the material movement group. To compare Atlanta's wage structures in 1991 and 1996, the wage distributions for the 20 jobs were aggregated into revised occupational groups.

Between 1991 and 1996, improving labor market conditions in Atlanta led to lower unemployment rates for all four groups. The unemployment rate for professional-technical workers fell from 2.6 percent in 1991 to 2.1 percent in 1996, from 3.3 percent to 2.5 percent for clerical workers, from 6.5 percent to 2.1 percent for skilled craft workers, and from 6.3 percent to 4.1 percent for transportation, material moving handlers, cleaners, helpers, and laborers. Other things being equal, our analysis suggest these falling rates of unemployment would be expected to raise average wage levels and to lower wage inequality in local occupational labor markets.

Table 7.1 reports data on these two variables for the re-defined occupational groups and for workers in all 20 job titles. Falling rates of unemployment did appear to contribute to rising real wages. The average log of the real wage rose sharply for the professional-technical group and more modestly for the other three groups. Overall, average real wages rose by about 7 percent for workers in the 20 jobs.

Falling unemployment rates may also have helped to reduce wage inequality within the technical, clerical, and craft groups. Wage

Table 7.1   The Wage Structure in Atlanta, 1991 and 1996

Group[a]	Number of workers	Mean ln(real wage)	Variance ln(real wage)
Professional-technical			
1991	11,259	2.1188	0.1469
1996	7,947	2.5833	0.1057
Office-clerical			
1991	14,316	2.0378	0.0741
1996	10,689	2.0437	0.0706
Skilled maintenance			
1991	3,827	2.2519	0.0905
1996	3,672	2.2685	0.0779
Material movement			
1991	24,769	1.7053	0.1651
1996	26,576	1,7412	0.1850
Overall			
1991	54,171	1.9177	0.1727
1996	48,884	1.9838	0.2363

SOURCE: Author's calculation from the 1991 Area Wage Survey data (BLS Bulletin 3060-14) and 1996 Occupational Compensation Survey data (BLS Bulletin 3085-25).

[a] The occupational groups contain fewer job titles than those used in the main body of this book. The professional-technical jobs are computer operator, computer programmer, computer system analyst, and drafter. The office clerical jobs are accounting clerk, key entry operator, secretary, switchboard receptionist, and word processor. The skilled maintenance jobs are general maintenance, maintenance electrician, maintenance machinist, maintenance mechanic, and motor vehicle mechanic. The material movement jobs are forklift operator, guard, janitor, order filler, shipping/receiving clerk, and truck driver.

inequality widened within the material movement group, however, as the real wages for truck drivers rose and those paid to guards, forklift operators, and shipper/receivers fell. Overall, wage inequality rose because the higher average real wage for the professional-technical group increased inequality between groups and because the material movement group, which shows rising inequality, weighs heavily in the calculation for average inequality within groups.

Still, the data suggest that some braking of the rise in wage inequality did accompany falling unemployment in Atlanta during the first half of the 1990s. Since U.S. unemployment rates fell further and remained very low into 1999, further research into the impact of tight labor markets on wage inequality and into comparative study of inequality trends in the 1980s and 1990s should be high on the agenda of labor economists.

Appendix A:
Data Sources and Definitions
of Metropolitan Areas

This appendix gives the boundaries for the local labor markets in the sample and notes the dates for the Area Wage Surveys and the Bureau of Labor Statistics Bulletin numbers containing the raw data for this study. In most cases, the definition of the local labor market is the same as the corresponding Metropolitan Statistical Area.

Anaheim is limited to Orange County, California, for every year. The AWS data are for October 1975 (Bulletin 1850-70), October 1978 (Bulletin 2025-65), October 1981 (Bulletin 3010-57), October 1984 (Bulletin 3025-58), and September 1988 (Bulletin 3045-43).

Atlanta consists of the following counties in Georgia for 1975 to 1984: Cherokee, Forsyth, Cobb, Gwinnett, Dekalb, Walton, Rockdale, Newton, Butts, Henry, Clayton, Fayette, Douglas, and Paulding. Barrow, Coweta, and Spalding counties were added in 1987. The AWS data are for May 1975 (Bulletin 1850-25), May 1978 (Bulletin 2025-28), May 1981 (Bulletin 3010-24), May 1984 (Bulletin 3025-18), May 1987 (Bulletin 3040-18), and May 1991 (Bulletin 3060-14).

Baltimore was originally defined to include Maryland's Anne Arundel, Baltimore, Carroll, Harford, and Howard counties. Queen Annes County was added in 1987. The AWS data are for August 1975 (Bulletin 1850-62), August 1978 (Bulletin 2025-50), August 1981 (Bulletin 3010-39), August 1984 (Bulletin 3025-39), September 1987 (Bulletin 3040-33), and September 1991 (Bulletin 3060-39).

Chicago consists of Cook, DuPage, Kane, Lake, McHenry, and Will counties in Illinois. After 1986, the definition was changed dramatically, so this study does not use post-1986 data for Chicago. The AWS data are for May 1974 (Bulletin 1795-27), May 1977 (Bulletin 1950-14), May 1980 (Bulletin 3000-26) , March 1983 (Bulletin 3020-10), and March 1986 (Bulletin 3035-9).

Cincinnati is defined as Clermont, Hamilton, and Warren counties in Ohio, plus Dearborn in Indiana, and Boone, Campbell, and Kenton counties in Kentucky for all years. The AWS data are for February 1974 (Bulletin 1795-16), July 1977 (Bulletin 1950-45), July 1979 (Bulletin 2050-28), July 1982 (Bulletin 3015-32), July 1985 (Bulletin 3030-29), and July 1989 (Bulletin 3050-27).

Cleveland is defined as Cuyahoga, Geauga, Lake, and Medina counties in Ohio. The AWS data are for September 1974 (Bulletin 1850-17), September 1977 (Bulletin 1950-53), September 1980 (Bulletin 3000-46), September 1983 (Bulletin 3020-46), September 1986 (Bulletin 3035-42), and September 1990 (Bulletin 3055-36).

Detroit includes Lapeer, Livingston, Macomb, Oakland, Wayne, and St. Clair counties in Michigan for 1976 to 1985 and adds Monroe County in 1989. The AWS data are for March 1976 (Bulletin 1900-15), March 1979 (Bulletin 2050-7), April 1982 (Bulletin 3015-15), April 1985 (Bulletin 3030-13), and December 1989 (Bulletin 3050-59).

Houston includes Brazoria, Ft. Bend, Harris, Liberty, and Montgomery counties in Texas for 1974, adds Waller County for 1977 to 1986, and deletes Brazoria County in 1990. The AWS data are for April 1974 (Bulletin 1795-22), August 1977 (Bulletin 1950-48), April 1980 (Bulletin 3000-18), May 1983 (Bulletin 3020-20), April 1986 (Bulletin 3035-20), and April 1990 (Bulletin 3055-17).

Indianapolis consists of the following Indiana counties for 1975 to 1988: Boone, Hamilton, Hancock, Hendricks, Johnson, Marion, and Shelby. The AWS data are for October 1975 (Bulletin 1850-66), October 1978 (Bulletin 2025-17), October 1981 (Bulletin 3010-56), October 1984 (Bulletin 3025-47), and October 1988 (Bulletin 3045-45).

Los Angeles is defined as Los Angeles County, California. The AWS data are for October 1975 (Bulletin 1850-86), October 1978 (Bulletin 2025-61), October 1981 (Bulletin 3010-66), October 1984 (Bulletin 3025-65), October 1986 (Bulletin 3035-53), and December 1989 (Bulletin 3050-57).

Miami is limited to Dade County, Florida. The AWS data are for October 1975 (Bulletin 1850-76), October 1978 (Bulletin 2025-60), October 1981 (Bulletin 3010-53), October 1984 (Bulletin 3025-48), October 1987 (Bulletin 3040-42), and October 1990 (Bulletin 3055-50).

Milwaukee is defined as Milwaukee, Ozaukee, Washington, and Waukesha counties in Wisconsin. The AWS data are for April 1975 (Bulletin 1850-21), April 1978 (Bulletin 2025-18), May 1981 (Bulletin 3010-16), May 1984 (Bulletin 3025-21), May 1987 (Bulletin 3040-17), and May 1991 (Bulletin 3060-15).

Minneapolis is defined for 1975 to 1984 as Anoka, Carver, Chisago, Dakota, Hennepin, Ramsey, Washington, and Wright counties in Minnesota and St. Croix County in Wisconsin. Isanti County, Minnesota, is added for 1987 and 1991. The AWS data are for January 1975 (Bulletin 1850-20), January 1978 (Bulletin 2025-2), January 1981 (Bulletin 3010-1), January 1984 (Bulletin 3025-2), February 1987 (Bulletin 3040-5), and February 1991 (Bulletin 3060-7).

Nassau–Suffolk includes Nassau and Suffolk counties in New York. The AWS data are for June 1975 (Bulletin 1850-39), June 1978 (Bulletin 2025-33), June 1981 (Bulletin 3010-31), August 1984 (Bulletin 3025-41), and August 1987 (Bulletin 3040-39).

New York includes Bronx, Kings, New York, Queens, Putnam, Richmond, Rockland, and Westchester counties in New York, and Bergen County in New Jersey from 1975 to 1985. Bergen County is deleted in 1989. The AWS data are for May 1975 (Bulletin 1850-45), May 1978 (Bulletin 2025-35), May 1981 (Bulletin 3010-41), May 1985 (Bulletin 3030-32), and June 1989 (Bulletin 3050-32).

Philadelphia is defined as Bucks, Chester, Delaware, Montgomery, and Philadelphia counties in Pennsylvania, and Burlington, Camden, and Gloucester counties in New Jersey. The AWS data are for November 1976 (Bulletin 1900-64), November 1979 (Bulletin 2050-57), November 1982 (Bulletin 3015-58), November 1985 (Bulletin 3030-64), and November 1988 (Bulletin 3045-57).

St. Louis includes Franklin, Jefferson, St. Charles, and St. Louis counties in Missouri and Clinton, Madison, Monroe, and St. Clair counties in Illinois for 1976 to 1985. Jersey County, Illinois, is added in 1989. The AWS data are for March 1976 (Bulletin 1900-19), March 1979 (Bulletin 2050-13), March 1982 (Bulletin 3015-11), March 1985 (Bulletin 3030-14), and March 1989 (Bulletin 3050-11).

San Diego is limited to San Diego County, California. The AWS data are for November 1974 (Bulletin 1850-13), November 1977 (Bulletin 1950-73), November 1980 (Bulletin 3000-71), Decmber 1983 (Bulletin 3020-70), December 1986 (Bulletin 3035-71), and December 1989 (Bulletin 3050-58).

San Jose consists of Santa Clara County, California. The AWS data are for March 1975 (Bulletin 1850-36), March 1978 (Bulletin 2025-9), March 1981 (Bulletin 3010-10), March 1984 (Bulletin 3025-15), and March 1988 (Bulletin 3045-13).

Seattle is defined as King and Snohomish counties in Washington. The AWS data are for January 1974 (Bulletin 1795-17), January 1977 (Bulletin 1950-12), December 1979 (Bulletin 2050-68), December 1982 (Bulletin 3015-72), December 1985 (Bulletin 3030-70), and November 1988 (Bulletin 3045-50).

Appendix B:
Wage Distribution Data

The basic data used in this study was taken from tables contained in the AWS reports. These tables list the number of workers in a specific job title receiving wages in each of 21 wage cells for office-clerical and professional-technical workers and in each of 22 wage cells for skilled maintenance and material movement workers. The AWS tables group the data for related job titles in a single table but do not aggregate the number of workers in a given wage cell across job titles. The data were not available from the Bureau of Labor Statistics in electronic form, which meant creating 444 spreadsheets containing the data for each occupational group in each metropolitan area for each period. This spreadsheet data was used to determine an aggregate wage distribution for each occupational group (note that the AWS tables do not provide totals across the job titles within each occupation) and then to create 111 spreadsheets, with the aggregate data for all four occupational groups for each metropolitan area for each year in the sample. The aggregate data by occupational group and by area was used in the analyses.

The wages for professional-technical workers and for office-clerical workers were reported in the AWS as weekly straight-time earnings. The weekly wages for the two groups were divided by the weighted average of standard weekly hours across the job titles in each occupational group in order to translate the wage data into hourly earnings cells for the workers in the two categories. To calculate means, medians, and wages at the 25th and 75th percentiles of the wage distribution, workers in all four occupational groups were assigned the midpoint of the wage range of the cell in which they were reported.

Midpoint wage levels for workers in the lowest and highest cells in the occupational tables were assigned in three ways. In most tables, the cells were closed, so the midpoint could be easily determined. In other tables, the highest and lowest cells were not closed, but footnotes permitted an estimation of their width and thus the determination of the midpoint. A minority of tables were not closed and did not have footnotes to help determine the width of the upper and lower cells. In those cases it was expedient to assume that those cells had the same range as the wage cells immediately adjacent in the table.

The median wage was estimated by interpolation, using the following formula (Abraham and Houseman 1995):

$$E_1 + [(0.50 - P_1) / (P_2 - P_1)] \times (E_2 - E_1)$$

where E_1 is the wage at the lower boundary of the cell containing the median, E_2 is the wage of the upper boundary of that cell, P_1 is the cumulative percentage of workers in the cells below that containing the median, and P_2 is the cumulative share of workers in the cells up to and containing the median wage. A similar approach was used to estimate the wage at the 25th and 75th percentiles of the occupational and the aggregate wage distributions for each area and period. To calculate those points in the aggregate distribution, a spreadsheet was used to rank workers from the four occupational groups by the midpoints of their wage cells. The variance was calculated as the sum of the squared deviations of the cell midpoints, from the weighted average of cell midpoints weighted, in turn, by the fraction of workers in each cell.

Appendix C:
Unemployment Rates

The data for the occupational unemployment rate are the yearly averages for 1976 to 1991 and were taken from annual issues of the *Geographic Profile of Employment and Unemployment*, published by the U.S. Bureau of Labor Statistics. The data show the unemployment rate by occupation for experienced workers and cover the last full-time job held for two or more weeks. There are two details to consider in this Appendix: first, the matching of occupations from the Area Wage Surveys with those in the *Geographic Profile*, and second, the method used to fill in for missing data.

The four occupational groups in the AWS are office-clerical, professional-technical, skilled maintenance, and material movement workers. These groups match well with four groups in the *Geographic Profile* for 1976 to 1982: clerical workers, professional and technical workers, craft and kindred workers, and nonfarm laborers. For 1983, however, the occupational groups were changed in the *Geographic Profile*, and the matching groups were then set as follows: data for professional specialty workers and technicians and related support workers were combined to match with the professional-technical group in the AWS; the administrative support group (including clerical workers) was matched with the office-clerical group in the AWS; the precision production, craft, and repair group was matched with the skilled maintenance worker group in the AWS; and the combined data for the transportation and material moving group and the handlers, equipment cleaners, helpers, and laborers group were matched with the AWS material movement group. Since the data used in this study are not continuous, no attempt was made to splice statistically the two sets of occupational unemployment rates. The first set of rates was used for the years up to 1982 and the second set for the years after 1982.

In a number of cases, the data on the unemployment rate for nonfarm laborers were not published. After 1983, the data for the combined occupations matched to the material movement group were not published. Unemployment rates were estimated in those cases. Employment in the occupation was calculated from other data published in the *Geographic Profile* on the distribution of employment by occupation. The number of unemployed workers was estimated as follows. First, the number of unemployed workers (from the occupational data) was subtracted from the total number of unemployed experienced workers to get a residual number of unemployed experienced workers for the community. Second, that residual number was allocated to occupations for which no data was reported by using the occupational distribution of the unemployed in the state in which the local labor market is centered. These estimates of unemployed and employed workers made it possible to calculate rates of occupational unemployment for cases where such data was not disclosed. A visual comparison of unemployment rates so estimated with those published for other metropolitan areas in the same year did not reveal the estimated unemployment rates to be beyond the range of values in the published data.

References

Abraham, Katharine G., and Susan N. Houseman. 1995. "Earnings Inequality in Germany." In *Differences and Changes in Wage Structures*, Richard B. Freeman and Lawrence F. Katz, eds. Chicago, Illinois: The University of Chicago Press, pp. 371–403.

Applebaum, Eileen, and Rosemary Batt. 1994. *The New American Workplace*. Ithaca, New York: ILR Press.

Autor, David H., Lawrence F. Katz, and Alan B. Krueger. 1997. *Computing Inequality: Have Computers Changed the Labor Market?* Working paper no. 5956, National Bureau of Economic Research, Cambridge, Massachusetts.

Baker, George, Michael Gibbs, and Bengt Holmstrom. 1994. "The Wage Policy of a Firm." *Quarterly Journal of Economics* 109(4): 921–955.

Barkume, Anthony J. 1996. "Does Proximity Link Job Markets? Some Comparisons between Occupations and Areas." *Compensation and Working Conditions* 1(3): 34–36.

Bartik, Timothy J. 1991. *Who Benefits from State and Local Economic Development Policies?* Kalamazoo, Michigan: W.E. Upjohn Institute for Employment Research.

———. 1994. "The Effects of Metropolitan Job Growth on the Size Distribution of Family Income." *Journal of Regional Science* 34(14): 483–501.

———. 1996. "The Distributional Effects of Local Labor Demand and Industrial Mix: Estimates Using Individual Panel Data." *Journal of Urban Economics* 40(2): 150–178.

Benedict, Mary Ellen, and Kathryn Shaw. 1995. "The Impact of Pension Benefits on the Distribution of Earned Income." *Industrial and Labor Relations Review* 48(5): 740–757.

Berman, Eli, John Bound, and Zvi Griliches. 1994. "Changes in the Demand for Skilled Labor within U.S. Manufacturing: Evidence from the Annual Survey of Manufactures." *Quarterly Journal of Economics* 109(2): 367–397.

Bernard, Andrew B., and J. Bradford Jensen. 1997. "Exporters, Skill Upgrading, and the Wage Gap." *Journal of International Economics* 42(1–2): 3–31.

Blackaby, D.H., K. Clark, D.G. Leslie, and P.D. Murphy. 1997. "The Distribution of Male and Female Earnings 1973–1991: Evidence for Britain." *Oxford Economic Papers* 49(2): 256–272.

Blanchflower, David G., and Andrew J. Oswald. 1994. *The Wage Curve.* Cambridge, Massachusetts: MIT Press.

Blau, Francine D., and Lawrence M. Kahn. 1994. "Rising Wage Inequality and the U.S. Gender Gap." *American Economic Review* 84(3): 23–28.

Block, Richard N., John Beck, and Daniel H. Kruger. 1996. *Labor Law, Industrial Relations and Employee Choice: The State of the Workplace in the 1990s.* Kalamazoo, Michigan: W.E. Upjohn Institute for Employment Research.

Borjas, George J., and Valerie A. Ramey. 1995. "Foreign Competition, Market Power and Wage Inequality." *Quarterly Journal of Economics* 110(4): 1075–1110.

Borjas, George J., Richard B. Freeman, and Lawrence F. Katz. 1996. "Searching for the Effect of Immigration on the Labor Market." *American Economic Review* 86(2): 246–251.

―――. 1997. "How Much Do Immigration and Trade Affect Labor Market Outcomes?" *Brookings Papers on Economic Activity* 1: 1–67.

Boskin, Michael J., Ellen R. Dulberger, Robert J. Gordon, Zvi Griliches, and Dale W. Jorgenson. 1997. "The CPI Commission: Findings and Recommendations." *American Economic Review* 87(2): 78–83.

Bound, John. 1996. Discussant on "The Role of Organizational Change and Labor Market Institutions." *New England Economic Review* (May/June special issue): 154–156.

Briggs, Vernon M. 1996. *Mass Immigration and the National Interest,* 2nd edition. Armonk, New York: M.E. Sharpe, Inc.

Buchinsky, Moshe. 1994. "Changes in the U.S. Wage Structure 1963–1987: Application of Quantile Regression." *Econometrica* 62(2): 405–458.

Buckberg, Elaine, and Alun Thomas. 1996. "Wage Dispersion in the 1980s: Resurrecting the Role of Trade through the Effects of Durable Employment Changes." *IMF Staff Papers* 43(2): 336–354.

Bureau of Labor Statistics. 1986. *BLS Measures of Compensation.* Bulletin 2239, Washington, D.C.: U.S. Government Printing Office.

Burtless, Gary. 1995. "International Trade and the Rise in Earnings Inequality." *Journal of Economic Literature* 33(2): 800–816.

Cappelli, Peter. 1996. "Technology and Skill Requirements: Implications for Establishment Wage Structures." *New England Economic Review* (May/June special issue): 139–153.

―――. 1993. "Are Skill Requirements Rising? Evidence from Production and Clerical Jobs." *Industrial and Labor Relations Review* 46(3): 515–530.

Card, David, and Alan B. Krueger. 1995. *Myth and Measurement: The New Economics of the Minimum Wage.* Princeton, New Jersey: Princeton University Press.

Card, David, and Thomas Lemieux. 1994. "Changing Wage Structure and Black–White Wage Differentials." *American Economic Review* 84(2): 29–33.

———. 1996. "Wage Dispersion, Returns to Skill, and Black-White Wage Differentials." *Journal of Econometrics* 74(2): 319–361.

Clark, W.A.V. 1996. "Scale Effects in International Migration to the United States." *Regional Studies* 30(6): 589–600.

Commission for Labor Cooperation. 1997. *North American Labor Markets· A Comparative Profile*. Dallas, Texas: Secretariat of the Commission for Labor Cooperation.

Constantine, Jill, and David Neumark. 1996. "Training and the Growth of Wage Inequality." *Industrial Relations* 35(4): 491–510.

Davis, Steve J., and John Haltiwanger. 1991. "Wage Dispersion between and within U.S. Manufacturing Plants, 1963–1986." In *Brookings Papers on Economic Activity, Microeconomics Annual*. Washington, D.C.: The Brookings Institution, pp. 115–180.

DiNardo, John, Nicole M. Fortin, and Thomas Lemieux. 1996. "Labor Market Institutions and the Distribution of Wages, 1973–1992: A Semiparametric Approach." *Econometrica* 64(5): 1001–1044.

DiNardo, John, and Thomas Lemieux. 1997. "Diverging Male Wage Inequality in the United States and Canada, 1981–1988: Do Institutions Explain the Difference?" *Industrial and Labor Relations Review* 50(4): 629–651.

Eberts, Randall W., and Joe A. Stone. 1997. *Wage and Employment Adjustment in Local Labor Markets*. Kalamazoo, Michigan: W.E. Upjohn Institute for Employment Research.

Eberts, Randall W., and Erica L. Groshen, eds. 1991. *Structural Changes in U.S. Labor Markets: Causes and Consequences*. Armonk, New York: M.E. Sharpe Inc.

Economic Report of the President. 1997. Washington, D.C.: U.S. Government Printing Orffice.

Feenstra, Robert C., and Gordon H. Hanson. 1996. "Globalization, Outsourcing, and Wage Inequality." *American Economic Review* 86(2): 240–245.

Ferrall, Christopher. 1995. "Levels of Responsibility in Jobs and the Distribution of Earnings among U.S. Engineers, 1961–1986." *Industrial and Labor Relations Review* 49(1): 150–169.

Freeman, Richard B. 1993. "How Much Has De-Unionization Contributed to the Rise in Male Earnings Inequality?" In *Uneven Tides: Rising Inequality in America*, Sheldon Danziger and Peter Gottschalk, eds. New York: The Russell Sage Foundation, pp. 133–163.

———. 1996. "Labor Market Institutions and Earnings Inequality." *New England Economic Review* (May/June special issue): 157–168.

————. 1997. *When Earnings Diverge: Causes, Consequences, and Cures for the New Inequality in the U.S.* Washington, D.C.: National Policy Association.

Freeman, Richard B., and Peter Gottschalk, eds. 1998. *Generating Jobs.* New York: The Russell Sage Foundation.

Gamboa Jr., Anthony M., David Gibson, and Gwendolyn Holland. 1994. *Analysis of Occupational Characteristics.* Revised ed., Louisville, Kentucky: Vocational Econometrics Press.

Gittleman, Maury. 1994. "Earnings in the 1980s: An Occupational Perspective." *Monthly Labor Review* 117(7): 16–27.

Gittleman, Maury, and Mary Joyce. 1996. "Earnings Mobility and Long-Run Inequality: An Analysis Using Matched CPS Data." *Industrial Relations* 35(2): 180–196.

Gittleman, Maury B., and David R. Howell. 1995. "Changes in the Structure and Quality of Jobs in the United States: Effects by Race and Gender, 1973–1990." *Industrial and Labor Relations Review* 48(3): 420–440.

Goldin, Claudia, and Robert A. Margo. 1992. "The Great Compression: The Wage Structure in the United States at Mid-Century." *Quarterly Journal of Economics* 107(1): 1–34.

Gottschalk, Peter. 1996. Discussant on "Labor Market Institutions and Earnings Inequality." *New England Economic Review* (May/June special issue): 169–172.

————. 1997. "Inequality, Income Growth, and Mobility: The Basic Facts." *The Journal of Economic Perspectives* 11(2): 21–40.

Gottschalk, Peter, and Robert Moffitt. 1994. "The Growth of Earnings Instability in the U.S. Labor Market." *Brookings Papers on Economic Activity* 2: 217–272.

Gottschalk, Peter, and Timothy M. Smeeding. 1997. "Cross-National Comparisons of Earnings and Income Inequality." *Journal of Economic Literature* 35(2): 633–687.

Gregg, Paul, and Alan Manning. 1997. "Skill-biased Change, Unemployment and Wage Inequality." *European Economic Review* 41(6): 1173–1200.

Grogger, Jeff, and Eric Eide. 1995. "Changes in College Skills and the Rise in the College Wage Premium." *Journal of Human Resources* 30(2): 280–310.

Groshen, Erica L. 1991a. "Sources of Intra-Industry Wage Dispersion: How Much Do Employers Matter?" *Quarterly Journal of Economics* 106(3): 869–883.

————. 1991b. "Five Reasons Why Wages Vary among Employers." *Industrial Relations* 30(3): 350–381.

————. 1996. *American Employer Salary Surveys and Labor Economics Research: Issues and Contributions.* Research paper no. 9604, Federal Reserve Bank of New York.

Hausman, Jerry A., Andrew W. Lo, and A. Craig MacKinlay. 1992. "An Ordered Probit Analysis of Transaction Stock Prices." *Journal of Financial Economics* 31(3): 319–379.

Haveman, Jon D. 1997. *The Effect of Trade Induced Displacement on Unemployment and Wages.* Working paper, Center for International Business Education and Research, Purdue University, West Lafayette, Indiana.

Haveman, Robert H., and Lawrence Buron. 1994. *The Anatomy of Changing Male Earnings Inequality: An Empirical Exploration of Determinants.* Working paper no. 104, The Jerome Levy Economics Institute, Annandale-on-Hudson, New York.

Head, Simon. 1996. "The New, Ruthless Economy." *The New York Review of Books*, February 29, pp. 47–52.

Hendry, D.F., A.R. Pagan, and J.D. Sargan. 1984. "Dynamic Specification." In *The Handbook of Econometrics*, Vol. 2, Z. Griliches and M.D. Intriligator, eds. Amsterdam: North Holland, pp. 1025–1100.

Horrigan, Michael W., and Ronald B. Mincy. 1993. "The Minimum Wage and Earnings and Income Inequality." In *Uneven Tides: Rising Inequality in America*, Sheldon Danziger and Peter Gottschalk, eds. New York: The Russell Sage Foundation, pp. 251–275.

Hotchkiss, Julie L. 1990. "Compensation Policy and Firm Performance: An Annotated Bibliography of Machine-Readable Data Files." *Industrial and Labor Relations Review* 43(3): 274-S–289-S.

Houseman, Susan N. 1995. *Job Growth and the Quality of Jobs in the U.S. Economy.* Working paper, W.E. Upjohn Institute, Kalamazoo, Michigan.

Howell, David R. 1994. *The Collapse of Low-Skill Male Earnings in the 1980s: Skill Mismatch or Shifting Wage Norms?* Working paper no. 105, The Jerome Levy Economics Institute, Annandale-on-Hudson, New York.

————. 1995. "Collapsing Wages and Rising Inequality: Has Computerization Shifted the Demand for Skills?" *Challenge* 38: 27–35.

Howell, David R., and Edward N. Wolff. 1991. "Trends in the Growth and Distribution of Skills in the U.S. Workplace, 1960–1985." *Industrial and Labor Relations Review* 44(3): 486–502.

————. 1992. "Technical Change and the Demand for Skill by U.S. Industries." *Cambridge Journal of Economics* 16(2): 127–146.

Hsiao, Cheng. 1996. *Analysis of Panel Data.* Cambridge, England: Cambridge University Press.

Hyclak, Thomas. 1996. "Structural Changes in Labor Demand and Unemployment in Local Labor Markets." *Journal of Regional Science* 36(4): 653–663.

Juhn, Chinhui, Kevin M. Murphy, and Brooks Pierce. 1993. "Wage Inequality and the Rise in Returns to Skill." *Journal of Political Economy* 101(3): 410–442.

Karoly, Lynn A. 1988. *A Study of the Distribution of Individual Earnings in the United States from 1967 to 1986.* Ph.D. dissertation, Yale University.

————. 1993. "The Trend in Inequality among Families, Individuals and Workers in the United States: A Twenty-Five Year Perspective." In *Uneven Tides: Rising Inequality in America*, Sheldon Danziger and Peter Gottschalk, eds. New York: The Russell Sage Foundation, pp. 19–97.

Karoly, Lynn A., and Jacob Alex Klerman. 1994. "Using Regional Data to Reexamine the Contribution of Demographic and Sectoral Changes to Increasing U.S. Wage Inequality." In *The Changing Distribution of Income in an Open U.S. Economy*, Jeffery H. Bergstrand, Thomas F. Cosemano, John W. Houck, and Richard G. Sheehan, eds. Amsterdam and New York: North Holland Press, pp. 183–216.

Katz, Lawrence F. 1996. "Shifts in Labor Demand and Supply." *New England Economic Review* (May/June special issue): 179–181.

Katz, Lawrence F., and Ana L. Revenga. 1989. "Changes in the Structure of Wages: The U.S. vs. Japan." *Journal of the Japanese and International Economies* 3(4): 209–75.

Krueger, Alan B. 1993. "How Computers Have Changed the Wage Structure: Evidence from Microdata, 1984–1989." *Quarterly Journal of Economics* 108(1): 33–60.

Krueger, Alan B., and Lawrence H. Summers. 1988. "Efficiency Wages and the Inter-Industry Wage Structure." *Econometrica* 56: 259–293.

Levy, Frank. 1995. "The Future Path and Consequences of the U.S. Earnings/Education Gap." *Economic Policy Review* 1(1): 35–41.

Levy, Frank, and Richard J. Murnane. 1992. "U.S. Earnings Levels and Earnings Inequality: A Review of Recent Trends and Proposed Explanations." *Journal of Economic Literature* 30(3): 1333–1381.

————. 1996. "With What Skills Are Computers a Complement?" *American Economic Review* 86(2): 258–262.

Linneman, Peter, Michael Wachter, and William Carter. 1990. "Evaluating the Evidence on Union Employment and Wages." *Industrial and Labor Relations Review* 44(1): 34–53.

Machin, Stephen. 1997. "The Decline of Labour Market Institutions and the Rise in Wage Inequality in Britain." *European Economic Review* 41 (3–5): 647–657.

Machin, S., A. Ryan, and J. Van Reenan. 1996. *Technology and Changes in Skill Structure: Evidence from an International Panel of Industries.* Discussion paper no. 297, Centre for Economic Performance, London, England, June.

McConnell, Margaret M., and Gabriel Perez Quiros. 1998. *Output Fluctuations in the United States: What Has Changed Since the Early 1980s?* Federal Reserve Bank of New York Staff Reports no. 41 (June).

Miller, Ann R., Donald J. Treiman, Pamela S. Cain, and Patricia A. Roos, eds. 1980. *Works, Jobs and Occupations. A Critical Review of the Dictionary of Occupational Titles.* Washington, D.C.: National Academy Press.

Mishel, Lawrence, and Jared Bernstein. 1996. "Did Technology's Impact Accelerate in the 1980s?" In *Proceedings of the Forty-Eighth Annual Meeting*, Industrial Relations Research Association, pp. 19–27.

Murnane, Richard J., John B. Willett, and Frank Levy. 1995. "The Growing Importance of Cognitive Skills in Wage Determination." *Review of Economics and Statistics* 77(2): 251–66.

Nelson, Richard R. 1990. "State Labor Legislation Enacted in 1989." *Monthly Labor Review* 113(1): 35–56.

———. 1991. "State Labor Legislation Enacted in 1990." *Monthly Labor Review* 114(1): 41–56.

———. 1992. "State Labor Legislation Enacted in 1991." *Monthly Labor Review* 115(1): 40–55.

Neumark, David, and William Wascher. 1992. "Employment Effects of Minimum and Subminimum Wages: Panel Data on State Minimum Wage Laws." *Industrial and Labor Relations Review* 46(1): 55–81.

Noponen, Helzi, Ann Markusen, and Karl Driessen. 1997. "Trade and American Cities." *Economic Development Quarterly* 11(1): 67–87.

Sachs, Jeffrey D., and Howard J. Shatz. 1996. "U.S. Trade with Developing Countries and Wage Inequality." *American Economic Review* 86(2): 234–239.

Schweitzer, Mark E. 1997. "Workforce Composition and Earnings Inequality." *Federal Reserve Bank of Cleveland Economic Review* 33(2): 13–24.

Scofea, Laura. 1986. "BLS Area Wage Surveys Will Cover More Areas." *Monthly Labor Review* 109(6): 19–23.

Special Reports Group. 1975. "Area Wage Survey Assessment—Interim Report (August)." Unpublished, Bureau of Labor Statistics.

Steindel, Charles. 1975. "Are There Good Alternatives to the CPI?" *Current Issues in Economics and Finance* 3(6): 1–5.

Stewart, M.B. 1995. "Union Wage Differentials in an Era of Declining Unionization." *Oxford Bulletin of Economics and Statistics* 57(2): 143–166.

Summers, Anita A. 1996. "A Statement of Our Concerns." *New England Economic Review* (May/June special issue): 173–176.

Teulings, Coen N. 1995. "The Wage Distribution in a Model of the Assignment of Skills to Jobs." *Journal of Political Economy* 103(2): 280–315.

Thornton, Robert J., and Jon T. Innes. 1989. "Interpreting Semilogarithmic Regression Coefficients in Labor Research." *Journal of Labor Research* 10(4): 443–447.

Topel, Robert H. 1997. "Factor Proportions and Relative Wages: The Supply-Side Determinants of Wage Inequality." *Journal of Economic Perspectives* 11(2): 55–74.

Uchitelle, Louis. 1997. "Raises Arrive at Bottom Rung of Labor Force." *New York Times*, May 23.

U.S. Bureau of Labor Statistics (various years). *Geographic Profile of Employment and Unemployment*. Washington, D.C.: U.S. Government Printing Office.

U.S. Department of Labor, Employment and Training Administration. 1991. *Dictionary of Occupational Titles*, 4th ed. Revised. Washington, D.C.: U.S. Government Printing Office.

Voos, Paula B., ed. 1994. *Contemporary Collective Bargaining in the Private Sector*. Madison, Wisconsin: Industrial Relations Research Association.

Wolff, Edward N. 1995. *Technology and the Demand for Skills*. Working paper no. 153, The Jerome Levy Economics Institute, Annandale-on-Hudson, New York.

Wood, Adrian. 1995. "How Trade Hurts Unskilled Workers." *Journal of Economic Perspectives* 9(3): 57–80.

Author Index

An italic *f*, *n*, or *t* following a page number means the cited name is in a *figure*, *note*, or *table*, respectively, on that page.

Subject Index

Note: An italic *f*, *n*, or *t* following a page number means the subject information is in a *figure*, *note*, or *table*, respectively, on that page.

About the Institute

The W.E. Upjohn Institute for Employment Research is a nonprofit research organization devoted to finding and promoting solutions to employment-related problems at the national, state, and local levels. It is an activity of the W.E. Upjohn Unemployment Trustee Corporation, which was established in 1932 to administer a fund set aside by the late Dr. W.E. Upjohn, founder of The Upjohn Company, to seek ways to counteract the loss of employment income during economic downturns.

The Institute is funded largely by income from the W.E. Upjohn Unemployment Trust, supplemented by outside grants, contracts, and sales of publications. Activities of the Institute comprise the following elements: 1) a research program conducted by a resident staff of professional social scientists; 2) a competitive grant program, which expands and complements the internal research program by providing financial support to researchers outside the Institute; 3) a publications program, which provides the major vehicle for disseminating the research of staff and grantees, as well as other selected works in the field; and 4) an Employment Management Services division, which manages most of the publicly funded employment and training programs in the local area.

The broad objectives of the Institute's research, grant, and publication programs are to 1) promote scholarship and experimentation on issues of public and private employment and unemployment policy, and 2) make knowledge and scholarship relevant and useful to policymakers in their pursuit of solutions to employment and unemployment problems.

Current areas of concentration for these programs include causes, consequences, and measures to alleviate unemployment; social insurance and income maintenance programs; compensation; workforce quality; work arrangements; family labor issues; labor-management relations; and regional economic development and local labor markets.

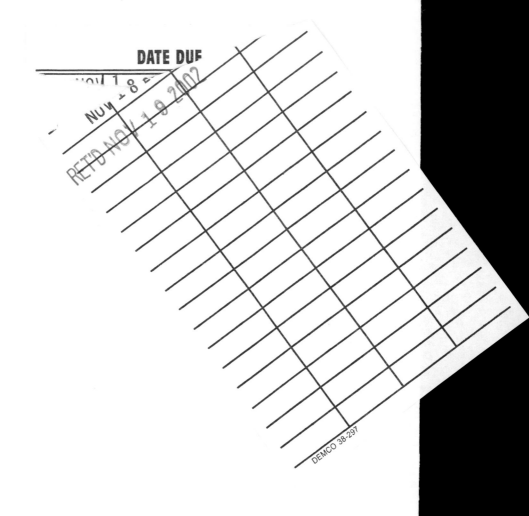